EVERGREEN GARDEN TREES
AND SHRUBS

EVERGREEN GARDEN TREES AND SHRUBS

IN COLOUR

English Editor: ANTHONY HUXLEY

Text adapted by DENIS HARDWICKE
and ALAN R. TOOGOOD

Illustrations by Verner Hancke

LONDON
BLANDFORD PRESS

First published in the English edition 1973
English text © 1973 Blandford Press Ltd.,
167 High Holborn, London, WC1V 6PH

World Copyright © 1972
Politikens Forlag A/S
Copenhagen

ISBN 07137 0621X

Colour section printed in Denmark by F. E. Bording A/S
Text set in Photon Times 9 pt by
Richard Clay (The Chaucer Press), Ltd., Bungay, Suffolk
and printed by Fletcher & Son Ltd., Norwich

CONTENTS

FOREWORD

This book will serve as a valuable reference for keen gardeners both in selection of shrubs and trees and their subsequent cultivation.

The general introduction covers the uses, suitability and treatment of the plants. Then follow the plates, arranged alphabetically according to the Latin names of the plants which are reproduced with the dimensional ratio of 3:5. They are numbered from 1 onwards and the descriptions follow the same order, with the number of the individual plant preceding the Latin name. The reference number therefore applies to both plate and text, and is used also in the index.

The descriptions, which come after the plates, give the name of the genus and species/variety, habitat, height and form of growth in cultivation (unless otherwise stated), and cultivation details.

Where English and American common names exist, these are given as well as the Latin names which have been brought up-to-date in accordance with Hillier's *Manual of Trees and Shrubs*.

Since experience has shown that frequently too many and too vigorously growing shrubs and trees are planted in gardens, scale drawings are given indicating the approximate height, breadth and form of growth in relation to an average house or adult. Thus the gardener in selecting and planting the shrubs and trees will know the size to which they can be expected to grow in the course of 20–30 years.

The selection of the plants has been made by the landscape architect, Eigil Kiaer. The editor of the English edition of this and the companion volume *Deciduous Garden Trees and Shrubs* is Anthony Huxley. The text has been prepared by Alan R. Toogood and Denis Hardwicke.

SOME USES OF EVERGREEN TREES AND SHRUBS

Most of the plants in this book will form permanent features in a garden and some, such as the conifers, have a very long life indeed. A conifer is a tree which bears cones and most of these are evergreen, among them the various pines, spruce, firs and cedars. There are, however, deciduous conifers, for instance Larch, Metasequoia and the Maidenhair Tree.

A tree has been defined as any woody plant with a distinct trunk or main stem, and a shrub as an ornamental plant with woody stems and branches, but without a tree-like trunk. A shrub may be any size from a few centimetres (inches) to 2 or 3 metres (6 to 10 feet) or more when fully grown.

It is most important when siting a tree or shrub to bear in mind its ultimate height and spread. Too often insufficient space is allowed when planting. Thus a young specimen Cedar about 45 cm (18 in.) high will eventually make a handsome tree 15 m (50 ft) in height with a spread of 9 m (30 ft) or more.

Obviously a young specimen tree will look somewhat lost if it is left to occupy a large space, but one can always plant bulbs and hardy perennials, or even sow annuals, to provide interest and colour while the more permanent tree or shrub is developing. Once planted, a tree or shrub should remain undisturbed for the rest of its life. It will resent being moved around so be sure that it is planted in the right place at the start. This may sound elementary, but in some gardens plants are moved so frequently that they give up the unequal struggle!

EVERGREEN FLOWERING SHRUBS

These combine all-the-year-round foliage value with colour at flowering time. Rhododendrons are probably the most widely planted for this purpose (150, 151, 153 and 163) and as long as the soil is lime-free and the position is reasonably sunny, they present little difficulty. They thrive best in a loamy soil or peat which retains moisture during the growing season. The soil should, however, be sufficiently well drained to take off any excess water, for they do not tolerate waterlogged conditions.

Camellias (178) flower from November to May and the blooms are therefore liable to damage by frost, but otherwise the plants are fairly hardy. They require similar soil to rhododendrons and these can be used as an effective background, not only to protect the camellia blooms from the early morning sun, which is most damaging after a frosty night, but at the same time to show up the shapely blooms to the best advantage. By making a careful selection of both rhododendrons and camellias it is possible to have a display lasting over three months.

TREES AND SHRUBS AS SPECIMEN PLANTS

Numerous trees and shrubs are seen at their best when grown as specimen plants or isolated from other subjects so that their beauty of form may be fully appreciated. The colour plates show clearly how many different types there are among the evergreen shrubs and trees: for instance, tall, slim, pagoda-shaped *Abies* and *Picea* species, *Pinus* with parasol-shaped, finely vaulted crowns, *Juniperus*, column-shaped and spherical, and the elegant *Chamaecyparis* and *Thuja* with a delicate drooping growth.

By careful siting at some focal point in the garden, say skilfully placed on a lawn, a tree or shrub will have ample space to develop naturally and not be forced to struggle upwards in search of light. This is too often the case when plants are overcrowded. This may happen with rhododendrons planted in a woodland setting where there are too many tall trees. Such shrubs, given more light, will remain much more compact and shapely, and few shrubs are more colourful than a well-grown rhododendron or, where space permits, a group of one variety, seen from the house across a well-kept lawn. Rhododendrons must, of course, have a lime-free soil, but otherwise they are not too fussy. Some are remarkably hardy and will provide shelter in the garden for smaller growing plants as well as an evergreen background.

Where space is limited, erect or fastigiate forms of trees and shrubs can prove useful. On a flat site two or three *Juniperus communis* 'Hibernica' (33) would lend height to a heather garden, as would the Golden Irish Yew, *Taxus baccata* 'Fastigiata Aureomarginata' (77). The low-growing Swiss Mountain Pine, *Pinus mugo* (64) associates happily with hardy heaths or it may be grown on top of a bank to form a spreading bush.

The Maidenhair Tree, *Ginkgo biloba* (26) is an attractive slow-growing Chinese tree of erect habit and is one of the small number of deciduous conifers. Its fan-shaped leaves are unique and turn a delightful clear yellow in the autumn. Also of erect habit, but requiring more space and moist, even boggy, conditions, is the Swamp Cypress, *Taxodium distichum* (75). This is an admirable specimen deciduous tree for planting beside a lake or stream and has good autumn colour. The comparatively recently introduced Dawn Redwood, *Metasequoia glyptostroboides* (47), is a fast-growing, deciduous conifer of erect habit which requires ample space to be seen at its best.

Among the evergreen conifers which are admirable as specimen trees beside or on a lawn are *Abies concolor* (3), which bears large cones; *Cedrus atlantica* 'Glauca' (9); *Cedrus deodara* (10); the European and Japanese Larch (44 and 45); the magnificent Weeping Spruce, *Picea breweriana* (51);

and *Picea pungens* 'Koster' (58), which makes an outstanding conical tree with branches down to ground level covered with silvery-blue needles.

There are many pines, some most decorative as specimen trees, others useful as windbreaks in coastal districts, such as the Shore or Beach Pine, *Pinus contorta* (61). Pines like an open sunny position and are not suitable for smokey, industrial areas. Some species thrive in poor soil, but the fine needled kinds are not usually happy on shallow chalky soil. *Pinus sylvestris* (71), the Scots Pine, is quite fast-growing in the early stages and makes an imposing specimen tree.

Those who attempt to grow Mimosa or Wattle (177) in the British Isles must have a really sheltered sunny position and a well-drained, preferably lime-free, soil. Some species will flower when quite young and are well worth trying against a south- or west-facing wall in the mildest districts. Or they may be grown in a tub and brought into a cool greenhouse for the winter, as may the various *Citrus* (179 to 181) and Pomegranate (197).

TREES AND SHRUBS FOR HEDGING

Some evergreens make ideal hedges. For this purpose they can be divided into two groups.

The first consists of the shrubs and trees which are used for the ordinary hedges, 180–200 cm (5 ft 11 in.–6 ft 7 in. high), that are usually the maximum height for divisions between houses in urban districts. The second consists of slower growing shrubs which are suitable for low hedges, say 50–100 cm (1 ft 7 in.–3 ft 3 in.) tall. Hedges such as these can provide good-looking evergreen frames to a flower garden, separate a kitchen garden from the rest of the garden or perhaps make a low hedge between the front garden and the road.

Abies alba (1), *A. nordmanniana* (5) and several other *Abies* species can be used as hedging, but cannot stand being trimmed too severely, so with these thick hedges must be anticipated, about 100 cm (3 ft 3 in.) at the bottom and 50 cm (1 ft 7 in.) at the top. This wedge shape is in fact the most appropriate for all hedges.

Juniperus communis 'Hibernica' (33) and *Juniperus communis* 'Suecica' (34) will because of their natural, slim habit provide a fine, thick hedge which hardly needs any trimming. They will only thrive in a light soil and in sunny position and are expensive to acquire.

Pinus contorta (61) and *P. mugo* (64) are suitable for making a thickset sheltering hedge in exposed places. They should be trimmed very lightly or not at all, but can be shaped carefully in the spring by pinching out the young shoots to half or two-thirds their length. This will encourage branching and give a thick, compact plant. One should not forget that such sheltering hedges take up a lot of room and can easily become 150–200 cm (4 ft 11 in.–6 ft 7 in.) thick.

The Yew, *Taxus baccata* (76), has for several centuries been used for hedges surrounding palaces and manor houses all over Europe, because this conifer is very suitable for making into square, tall hedges, pyramids or hemispheres by clipping.

In the average somewhat small, present-day gardens, Yew is hardly the most suitable plant for making hedges. It must have room to grow to quite a considerable thickness. Also Yew hedges—the same goes for most evergreen hedges—are very sensitive and easily damaged by shrubs and perennials planted too near them, which can cause holes and withered places. But all the same one should not entirely exclude the use of Yew for hedging, especially because of its tranquil, dark green colour. In a garden of some size, Yew is certainly the most handsome plant to create a calm frame for a mass of colourful flowers. Hollies (*Ilex*) (129–131) are good for thick, impenetrable hedges, but of course clipping may prove painful because of the prickly leaves. Dense hedges can also be made from *Prunus laurocerasus* (143).

Thuja is perhaps the conifer most suitable for evergreen hedges. All the *Thuja* species can be used with the exception perhaps of *T. standishii* (81), since the beauty of its very special form of growth when planted free standing would be spoilt by clipping. The most suitable is *T. occidentalis* 'Fastigiata' (84), which on account of its natural, slim, close way of growing will rapidly produce tall, good-looking hedges. The original species, *T. occidentalis* (82), is also suitable for tall hedges, but must be slipped annually in August. It will produce a wider hedge than the others.

Hedges are not necessarily grown to enclose a garden. There are other reasons too. Nothing can set off the noble form and beautiful colour of lilies, tulips and roses like a background consisting of Box, Cherry Laurel or Yew.

In some gardens a low, evergreen hedge may be planted to make a frame for a group of beautiful flowers. It is common practice in modern gardens to have special areas devoted, for example, to roses of various kinds, or perennials of all sorts, or bulbs, instead of planting these all over the garden.

To enclose such individual gardens with low, perhaps free-growing hedges, various species of *Berberis* can be recommended, such as *Berberis buxifolia* 'Nana' (93), *B. julianae* (96) and *B. verruculosa* (98), which all grow evenly and can stand being clipped with care in August. Box (*Buxus*) (99–102) can be used for hedges from 15 cm (6 in.) upwards; there is no better evergreen shrub for producing solid hedges around a flower garden. The evergreen *Cotoneaster* species *C. microphyllus* (109) and *C. hybridus* 'Skogsholmen' (112) are, like the semi-evergreen *Pyracantha coccinea*, also very suitable, and this is equally true of privets such as *Ligustrum vulgare* (134) and *Lonicera pileata* (135).

TOWN ATMOSPHERE AND SHADE

Few conifers can tolerate town atmosphere and growing in the shade. Both Spruce and Pine will rapidly become thin-crowned and sickly looking if they are planted under or among thick-canopied deciduous trees such as the Horse Chestnut, Poplar and Elm, which impoverish the soil. The most suitable conifers to grow in shady places are *Taxus* (76) and its many varieties. *Thujopsis dolabrata* (86) can also tolerate fairly deep shade and smoke-filled atmosphere; *Thuja occidentalis* (82) and its varieties can stand some shade, but dislike town atmosphere.

Among the broad-leaved evergreen shrubs and trees, the large-leaved *Buxus sempervirens* 'Bullata' (102) should be singled out for special mention since it can put up with an extraordinary amount of shade and polluted air, but it will impoverish the soil. The hardy *Aucuba japonica* 'Viridis' (92), holly, *Ilex aquifolium* (129) and *Prunus laurocerasus* (143–144) can also be recommended.

Among the low-growing, broad-leaved evergreen shrubs *Euonymus fortunei* (120–122) and *Mahonia aquifolium* (136) can tolerate plenty of shade. To cover the ground in the most shady places there are different forms of Ivy (*Hedera*) (125–127) and Periwinkle (*Vinca*) (174–176).

Rose of Sharon, *Hypericum calycinum* (128), is also very good for this purpose.

COASTAL CONIFERS

When planting shrubs and trees on the coast many people are tempted to buy species which cannot tolerate conditions such as high winds, poor, sandy soil and salt spray. The choice of conifers that can tolerate these severe conditions is very limited and they should be supplemented by various deciduous shrubs and trees, which are dealt with in the companion volume.

Picea sitchensis (59) is a conifer which can be warmly recommended since it is very wind-resistant, whereas *Picea pungens* (56) cannot tolerate quite so much wind and sea mist, although it will thrive in a poor sandy soil. *Pinus contorta* (61) can be planted near the beach but will, as the name suggests, become contorted and possibly scorched if planted too near the sea. *Pinus mugo* (64) can tolerate poor sandy soil and winds, but not salt spray. Practically all the good-looking *Juniperus* species are resistant to both wind and poor soil. *J. communis* and its many varieties (31–34) can especially be recommended for beach conditions.

None of the broad-leaved evergreen shrubs and trees can really be recommended for this purpose. The result will only be contorted plants with small leaves that may be scorched by frost in the spring.

PLANTING

To give a tree or shrub the best possible start in life the soil should be thoroughly dug—do not bring the subsoil to the surface but break it up with a fork if necessary—for the majority of trees and shrubs like to make deep roots and thus benefit during periods of drought when the surface soil is arid. Ideally, the ground should be dug a week or so before planting, to give the soil time to settle.

This may not always be feasible and with newly dug soil it will be all the more important to make the plant firm in the ground after spreading out the roots as much as possible in the hole. This is usually done by pressing down firmly but gently with the heel of your boot as the soil is being replaced. When shovelling the soil back, joggle the tree up and down a few times to ensure that the soil gets between the roots.

Where a standard tree is being planted, it may be wise to give it support with a stake or stout cane. The stake should be put in position in the middle of the hole before planting and not driven into the ground beside the tree after planting as this may damage the tree roots. Where several trees are to be planted this method has the added advantage of getting the distances between each tree correct. It is easy to move a stake, but not a tree.

It is important that when the tree is finally planted the level of the soil around the stem is the same as before it was transplanted. Avoid burying too deep or leaving the tree almost sitting on the surface.

If the ground is poor and sandy, or very heavy, it is wise to fork in some garden compost, leafmould or peat when the ground is being initially prepared. Heavy clay soil may also need gravel or coarse grit. Use also a high-value balanced fertiliser, say N.12 P.18 K.12 (that is, 12% nitrogen, 18% phosphate, 12% potash) at 2 oz per tree at least.

You should also make sure there is not a high water-table during the winter months in the place where you intend to plant. Should newly planted shrubs and trees stand with their roots in water right through the winter, you can expect that many of them will have died by the spring.

Some shrubs must have a lime-free soil—rhododendrons, camellias, some varieties of hardy heathers and various other ericaceous plants, as indicated in the text later—so do not attempt to grow these where there is chalk in the soil. Such plants can, of course, be grown in tubs or other sizable containers filled with a lime-free compost and will make most decorative features for a terrace, patio garden or a roof garden so long as it is not too exposed. Such containers must not be allowed to dry out and watering is essential in dry spells.

Apart from providing the plants with the soil they require, it is also very necessary to guard against frost getting into the soil. This is done by covering the soil around the plants with a 10–15 cm (4–6 in.) layer of dead leaves and peat. As a further precaution to prevent the covering blowing away, lay fir branches across.

PRUNING AND TRIMMING

Very few conifers can be pruned, since they cannot produce new branches where they have been trimmed. On the other hand the young soft shoots can

14

be pinched off in May or June if a compact, close growth is required. This process of pinching off, which consists of cutting off about half or a little more of the young shoots, will quickly produce numerous side shoots which have time to mature before the winter.

A few of the spruces can withstand severe pruning, as for example the Sitka Spruce, and are therefore suitable as hedges. *Cryptomeria*, *Chamaecyparis*, *Juniperus* and *Thuja* species can be trimmed in the spring, but this should be done with great care and understanding so as not to spoil their characteristic shapes.

As already noted, several evergreens make good hedges. These will need periodic clipping or trimming. Fairly fine-leaved species such as yew (*Taxus*), holly (*Ilex*), box (*Buxus*), privets (*Ligustrum* and *Lonicera*) can be trimmed with shears or powered hedge trimmers. Although these can be used on broad-leaved evergreens such as Cherry laurel (*Prunus laurocerasus*), they will leave bisected leaves which go brown, and the use of secateurs may be preferable, at any rate to tidy up after trimming.

PESTS AND DISEASES

There are very many kinds of insect that will attack evergreen trees and shrubs, but they are unlikely to cause more than temporary disfigurement, and attacked trees usually grow out of this the following year. In any event, there is not much to be done in the case of large trees. It is in the first few years after planting that insect attack can cripple trees, and a watch should be kept on them: they will still be small enough for spraying with an appropriate insecticide to be effective. A broad-spectrum insecticide, perhaps containing BHC, malathion and the systemic rogor, should deal with almost any insect pest. Sevin dust will control caterpillars.

If rabbits or deer are known to be in your locality and likely to enter the garden, the trunks of trees must be protected, or these animals may gnaw the bark, and this is likely to kill the tree. Special wrap-round spiral protectors are readily available.

Diseases are usually caused by various kinds of fungi. They may be relatively superficial, like mildew and rust, or internal, like Dutch elm disease and honey fungus. There is very little to be done about any of these on a garden scale, but any wound caused by branch cutting or breaking should be painted with an antiseptic tree-wound dressing to prevent entry of fungus spores. Tree planting in the vicinity of old stumps should be avoided; at least the stumps and as much of their roots as possible should be removed.

BIBLIOGRAPHY

Adrian Bloom, *Conifers for your Garden* (Floraprint, 1972). Available only from Bressingham Gardens, Diss, Norfolk.

George E. Brown, *The Pruning of Trees, Shrubs and Conifers* (Faber and Faber, 1972)

Geoffrey Chadbund, *Flowering Cherries* (Collins, 1972)

H. Edland, *The Pocket Encyclopaedia of Roses in Colour* (Blandford, 4th revised edn. 1973)

H. L. Edlin, *Guide to Tree Planting and Cultivation* (Collins, 1970, 1972)

Richard Gorer, *Multi-Season Shrubs and Trees* (Faber and Faber, 1971)

H. G. Hillier, *Hillier's Manual of Trees and Shrubs* (David and Charles, 1972)

Roy Hudson, *The Pruning Handbook* (Blandford, 1967)

Anthony Huxley, *Deciduous Garden Trees and Shrubs in Colour* (Blandford, 1973)

Eigil Kiaer, *Garden Shrubs and Trees in Colour* (Blandford, revised edn. 1973)

A. F. Mitchell, *Conifers in the British Isles* (H.M.S.O., 1972) Forestry Commission Booklet No. 33

Terry Underhill, *Heaths and Heathers* (David and Charles, 1972)

H. J. Welch, *Dwarf Conifers* (Faber and Faber, 1966)

CONIFERS

1. **Abies alba**
   European Silver Fir
a. Cone

2. **Abies balsamea**
   Balsam Fir

1   2

3　　　　　　　3 a

5

3. Abies concolor
Colorado Fir
White Fir
a. Cone

4. Abies grandis
Giant Fir

5. Abies nordmanniana
Caucasian Fir,
Nordmann Fir

4   3   5

6

7

6. **Abies procera** 'Glauca'
   Blue Noble Fir

7. **Abies pinsapo**
   'Glauca'
   Blue Spanish Fir

8. **Araucaria araucana**
   Monkey-puzzle Tree,
   Chile Pine

8

7   8   6

9

10

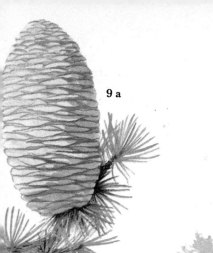

9 a

9. Cedrus atlantica
'Glauca'
Blue Atlas Cedar
a. Young cone

10. Cedrus deodara
Deodar, Cedar

10   9

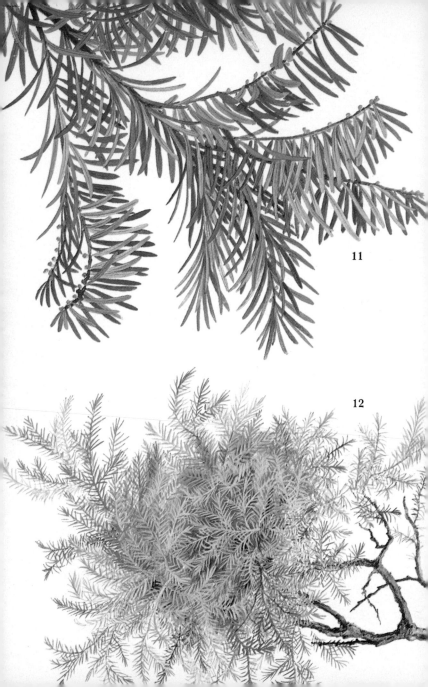

11

12

11. **Cephalotaxus harringtonia drupacea**
Cow's Tail Pine, Japanese Plum-yew

12. **Chamaecyparis pisifera** 'Squarrosa'
Moss Sawara or False Cypress

12   11

13. **Chamaecyparis lawsoniana**
    'Allumii'
    Allum's Cypress

14. **Chamaecyparis lawsoniana**
    'Aureovariegata'

16   18   13   14

15. **Chamaecyparis lawsoniana**
    'Fletcheri'

16. **Chamaecyparis lawsoniana**
    'Stewartii'

17. **Chamaecyparis lawsoniana**
    'Triomphe de Boskoop'

18. **Chamaecyparis nootkatensis**
    'Pendula'
    Weeping Nootka Cypress,
    False Cypress

18

19

20

19. Chamaecyparis obtusa 'Nana'
Dwarf Hinoki
Cypress, Dwarf
False Cypress

20. Chamaecyparis pisifera 'Aurea'

21. Chamaecyparis pisifera 'Filifera' Thread Sawara, False Cypress

21

21   19   20

22. Cryptomeria japonica 'Elegans'
Japanese Cedar, Plume Cryptomeria

23. Cryptomeria japonica 'Lobbii'
Lobb's Japanese Cedar

22

23

24

25

24. Cryptomeria japonica 'Cristata'

25. Cunninghamia lanceolata
Chinese Fir

24   25

26. Ginkgo biloba
Maidenhair
Tree
a. Fruit

26

26 a

26   26

27

30

27. **Juniperus chinensis**
    Chinese Juniper

28. **Juniperus × media (chinensis) 'Blaauw'**

29. **Juniperus × media (chinensis)**
    'Pfitzerana'
    Pfitzer Juniper

30. **Juniperus media plumosa aurea**
    Creeping Juniper, Golden Plume Chinese
    Juniper

28

29

31

32 a

32

31. **Juniperus communis**
   'Hornibrookii'

32. **Juniperus communis** 'Repanda'
   a. Berries

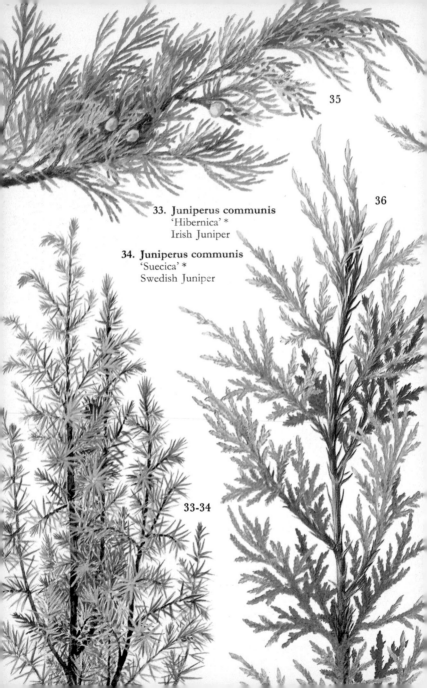

35

36

33. Juniperus communis
'Hibernica' *
Irish Juniper

34. Juniperus communis
'Suecica' *
Swedish Juniper

33-34

35. Juniperus sabina
Savin Juniper

37

36. Juniperus sabina 'Hicksii'

37. Juniperus sabina tamariscifolia
Spanish Juniper, Tamarix Savin
Juniper

* Nos. 33 and 34 differ only in the growth form

38. **Juniperus squamata**
'Meyeri'

39. **Juniperus virginiana**
'Elegantissima'
Pencil Cedar

40. Juniperus virginiana
'Glauca'

41. Juniperus 'Grey Owl'

42. Juniperus excelsa
'Stricta Albo-variegata'
Variegated Spiny or Greek Juniper

43. Juniperus horizontalis 'Glauca'
Creeping Juniper
Different forms of **Juniperus**

42

43

Some forms of **Juniperus**

44

45

46

44. Larix decidua
European Larch

45. **Larix kaempferi**
Japanese Larch

46. Libocedrus decurrens
(**Calocedrus**
decurrens)
Incense Cedar

45   44

47

47. Metasequoia glyptostroboides
Dawn Redwood

48

48 a

50

49

48. **Picea abies**
   Norway Spruce
 a. Cone

49. **Picea asperata**
   Dragon Spruce

50. **Picea glauca**
   White Spruce

48   50   49

51

52

51. Picea breweriana
Brewer's Weeping
Spruce

**52. Picea glauca
albertiana** 'Conica'

57

54

53. Picea abies 'Nidiformis'

54. Picea omorika
Serbian Spruce

55

53

56

55. **Picea orientalis**
Oriental Spruce

56. **Picea pungens**
Colorado Spruce

57. **Picea pungens**
'Moerheimii'

53   54   56

58

59

59 a

58. Picea pungens 'Koster'
Koster's Blue Spruce

59. Picea sitchensis
Sitka Spruce
a. Cone

58   59   59

60

60 a

61

60. Pinus cembra
Arolla or Swiss
Stone Pine
a. Cone

61. Pinus contorta
Shore or Beach
Pine

**62. Pinus wallichiana
(griffithii)**
Bhutan or
Himalayan Pine

63 a

63

63. Pinus jeffreyi
Jeffrey's Pine
a. Cone

64

64. Pinus mugo
Swiss Mountain
Pine

65. Pinus nigra
Austrian Pine
a. Cone

65

65 a

65

64

66

66. **Pinus parviflora**
Japanese White Pine

67. **Pinus parviflora**
'Glauca'

67

67   66

69 a

69

68. Pinus peuce
Macedonian Pine

69. Pinus ponderosa
Western Yellow or
Ponderosa Pine
a. Cone

71

70 a

70. Pinus strobus
Eastern White or
Weymouth Pine
a. Cone

71. Pinus sylvestris
Scots Pine

72

72 a

72. Pseudotsuga menziesii
Pacific Coast or
Oregon
Douglas Fir
a. Cone

73 a

73

73. Sequoiadendron giganteum
Wellingtonia,
Giant Sequoia
a. Cone

73

74. Sciadopitys verticillata
Umbrella Pine

75. Taxodium distichum
Swamp
or Common Bold
Cypress

74

75

79

78

76

76. Taxus baccata
English Yew

77. **Taxus baccata**
'Fastigiata Aureomarginata'
Golden Irish Yew

78. **Taxus baccata** 'Stricta'
('Fastigiata')
Irish Yew

79. **Taxus cuspidata**
Japanese Yew

77

78 76 Clipped forms of **Taxus baccata**

80. Thuja plicata
Western Red Cedar or
Giant Arborvitae

81. Thuja standishii
Japanese Arborvitae

81   80   80

82

82. Thuja occidentalis
American Arborvitae

83. Thuja occidentalis
'Ellwangerana'

84. Thuja occidentalis
'Fastigiata'

84

83

82   84   82 82

87

85. **Thuja occidentalis**
'Douglasii'

86. **Thujopsis dolabrata**
Hiba False Arborvitae

87. **Torreya nucifera**
Japanese Torreya

85   86   87

88

89

88. **Tsuga canadensis**
Canada or Eastern
Hemlock

89. **Tsuga heterophylla**
Western Hemlock

90

90. Tsuga diversifolia
Northern Japanese
Hemlock

EVERGREEN TREES
AND SHRUBS

92

91

91. Aucuba japonica 'Crotonifolia'
Variegated Japanese Aucuba,
Spotted Laurel

92. Aucuba japonica 'Viridis'

93. Berberis buxifolia 'Nana'
Dwarf Magellan Barberry

94. Berberis candidula
Paleleaf Barberry

95. Berberis gagnepainii
Black Barberry

96

98

97

96. **Berberis julianae**
   Wintergreen Barberry

97. **Berberis stenophylla**
   Rosemary Barberry

98. **Berberis verrucul**
   Warty Barberry

99. **Buxus sempervire**
   Common Box

99

102

100. Buxus sempervirens
'Marginata'

101

100

101. Buxus sempervirens
'Aureovariegata'

102. Buxus sempervirens 'Bullata'

103

106

105

107

104

103. Calluna vulgaris
Heather, Ling

104. Calluna vulgaris 'Alba Plena'

105. Calluna vulgaris 'H. E. Beale'

106. Calluna vulgaris 'Mair's Variety'

107. Calluna vulgaris 'C. W. Nix'

108

108. Cotoneaster dammeri
Bearberry Cotoneaster

109. Cotoneaster microphyllus
Small-leaved Cotoneaster

109

111

110. Cotoneaster salicifolius floccosus

111. Cotoneaster × watereri

110

112

112. Cotoneaster 'Skogsholmen'

113. Daphne cneorum
Garland Flower or Rose Daphne

113

. × **darleyensis**
ley Heath

Erica × **darleyensis**
'Silberschmelze' ('Molten Silver')

118

119

114.

117.

116.

115.

116. Erica carnea 'Vivellii'

117. Erica carnea 'Winter Beauty'

118. Erica tetralix 'Alba Praecox'
Variety of Cross-leaf Heath

119. Erica vagans 'Mrs. D. F. Maxwell'
Variety of Cornish Heath

121

122

123

120. Euonymus fortunei 'Variegatus' ('Gracilis')

121. Euonymus fortunei radicans

120

124

122. Euonymus fortunei 'Vegetus'

123. Gaultheria procumbens
Checkerberry or Wintergreen

124. Hebe armstrongii

125

126

127 a

127

128

129

125. **Hedera colchica** 'Dentata'
Persian or Colchis Ivy

126. **Hedera colchica** 'Dentata
Variegata'

127. **Hedera helix**
Common Ivy
a. Flowering shoot

128. **Hypericum calycinum**
Rose of Sharon, Aaronsbeard,
St. John's Wort

129. **Ilex aquifolium**
Common Holly

130. Ilex aquifolium 'Aureomarginata
    Ovata'

131. Ilex pernyi
    Perny Holly

132. Kalmia latifolia
    Mountain Laurel
    a. Flower cluster

134. **Ligustrum vulgare**
Common Privet

133

133. **Lavandula spica (officinalis)**
Lavender

132 a

135

136 b

135. Lonicera pileata
Privet Honeysuckle

36. Mahonia aquifolium
  Oregon Grape,
  Holly Grape
  a. Young foliage
  b. Fruit

37. Osmanthus heterophyllus
  Holly Osmanthus

136 a

136

137

139

139 a

139 b

138

138. Pachysandra terminalis
Japanese Spurge, Japanese
Pachysandra

139. Pernettya mucronata
Chilean Pernettya
a. and b. Berries

140. Pieris japonica
Japanese Andromeda

141. Pieris 'Forest Flame'

142. Pieris japonica 'Dorothy
Wycoff'

143

143. Prunus laurocerasus
Common or Cherry Laurel

144. Prunus laurocerasus
'Schipkaensis'

149

148

145. Rhododendron ferrugineum
Alpenrose or
Rock Rhododendron

146. Rhododendron × halense
'Hardyzer Beauty'

146

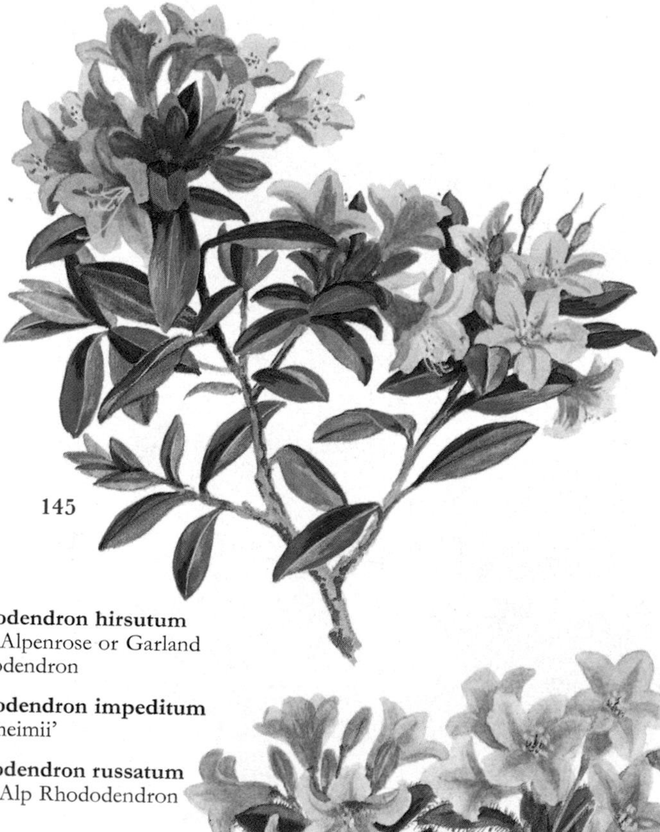

145

Rhododendron hirsutum
Tyrol Alpenrose or Garland
Rhododendron

Rhododendron impeditum
'Moerheimii'

Rhododendron russatum
Royal Alp Rhododendron

147

150

151

150. **Rhododendron**
'Cunningham's White'

151. **Rhododendron** 'Jewel'

152. **Rhododendron impeditum**
Cloudland Rhododendron

153. **Rhododendron wardii**
Ward Rhododendron

152

153

154. **Rhododendron catawbiense** 'Album'

155. **Rhododendron catawbiense** 'Grandiflorum'

156. **Rhododendron** 'Doncaster'

157. **Rhododendron** 'Hugh Koster'

158. **Rhododendron** 'Cunningham's Blush'

159. **Rhododendron** 'Davies Evans'

160. **Rhododendron** 'Purple Splendour'

163

161

162

164

165

164. **Arundinaria japonica**
    (Pseudosasa japonica)
    Metake

165. **Arundinaria murieliae**

166. **Arundinaria nitida**

166

167

167 b

167 a

168

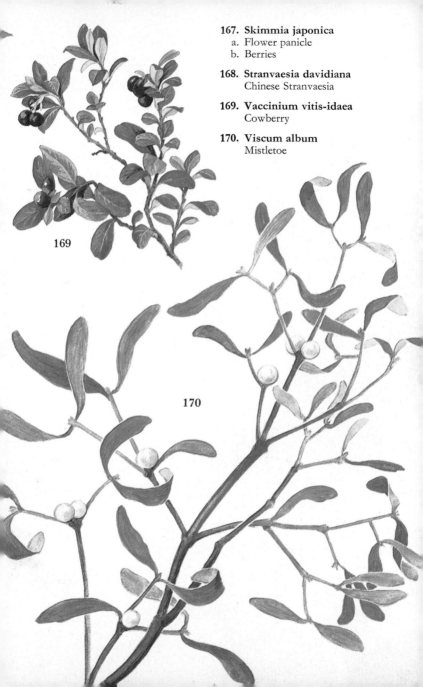

167. Skimmia japonica
  a. Flower panicle
  b. Berries

168. Stranvaesia davidiana
Chinese Stranvaesia

169. Vaccinium vitis-idaea
Cowberry

170. Viscum album
Mistletoe

169

170

173

171

171. Viburnum × burkwoodii
Burkwood Viburnum

172. **Viburnum davidii**
David Viburnum

173. **Viburnum rhytidophyllum**

174. **Vinca minor**
Lesser Periwinkle

172

174

175. Vinca major
Greater Periwinkle

176. Vinca major
'Variegata'

EVERGREEN TREES AND SHRUBS
HARDY IN SOUTHERN EUROPE

177

177. **Acacia cyanophylla**
Blue-leaved Wattle

178. **Camellia japonica** hybrids
Red and white forms

178

179

179. Citrus sinensis
Sweet Orange

180. Citrus limonia
Lemon

181. Citrus nobilis (reticulata)
King Orange, Mandarin,
Tangerine

181   180   179   180   179

180

181

182

183

183 a

182. Cupressus sempervirens
Mediterranean or Italian Cypress

183. Eriobotrya japonica
Loquat
a. Fruit

184. Eucalyptus globulus
Tasmanian Blue Gum
a. Fruit

184

184 a

185. Jasminum floridum Jasmine

186

185

186. Laurus nobilis
Bay Laurel, Sweet Bay
a. Clipped forms in tubs

187. Myrtus communis
Myrtle
a. Myrtle wreath

187

187 a

188. Myrtus communis
'Romana'

188

186 a

189

0. Olea europaea
Common Olive
a. Flowering stem
b. Fruit

190

190 a

190 b

193

191

191. Phoenix canariensis
Canary Island Date Palm

192. **Chamaerops humilis**
Mediterranean Fan Palm

193. **Jubaea spectabilis**
Coquito Palm,
Chilean Wine Palm

194. **Washingtonia filifera**
California Fan Palm

195
195 a

196

195. Pinus pinea
Umbrella Pine or
Italian Stone Pine
a. Cone

197

197a

196. Pittosporum tobira
Japanese Pittosporum

198

197. Punica granatum
Pomegranate
a. Ripening fruit

198. Quercus ilex
Holly or Holm Oak

199. Rosmarinus officinalis
Rosemary

200. Viburnum tinus
Laurustinus

199

200

DESCRIPTIVE AND CULTURAL NOTES

CONIFERS

1. Abies alba

European Silver Fir

Height 30 m (100 ft). Originates from the mountainous regions of central Europe where it may be considerably taller. This imposing erect tree has smooth greyish-white bark and spreading, opposite branches. The solitary cylindrical cones are up to 18 cm (7 in.) long. Grows well in deep, moist soil and in districts, such as western Scotland, where there is a heavy rainfall. It is one of the few firs that will tolerate shade; it will not grow in hot, dry conditions. Young trees are liable to be damaged by late spring frost in exposed parts of the British Isles.

2. Abies balsamea

Balsam Fir

Height 25 m (80 ft). A slow-growing North American species with strongly balsam-scented leaves. The purple-violet cones with velvety scales are cylindrical and up to 10 cm (4 in.) long. This tree will not tolerate lime and is not widely planted. Of much more interest to the gardener is the dwarf form 'Hudsonia' with an eventual height and spread of about 1 m (3 ft) and an annual growth of about 2·5 cm (1 in.). The foliage is dark green but the young shoots are a pale soft green. It does not produce cones. A charming, compact evergreen for the rock garden.

3. Abies concolor

White or Colorado Fir

Height 15 m (50 ft). A handsome tree from the Rocky Mountains of the western United States where it may be considerably taller. The smooth grey bark becomes grooved in mature specimens. The cylindrical cones are pale green when young becoming brownish-purple, up to 13 cm (5 in.) long. Thrives in ordinary well-drained soil and in a sunny open position.

4. Abies grandis

Giant Fir

Height 50 m (150 ft). A beautiful species from California to the Columbia River reaching a height of 100 m (300 ft) on Vancouver Island. The horizontally disposed leaves are an attractive olive-green. Cones bright green up to 20 cm (8 in.) long. Tolerant of lime in moderation and likes a well-drained, moist soil. Does best in areas with a heavy rainfall.

5. Abies nordmanniana

Nordmann or Caucasian Fir

Height 30 m (100 ft). An imposing native of Caucasus and Asia Minor with tiered branches sweeping downwards. The cones are greenish when young, becoming dark brown, cylindrical, up to 18 cm (7 in.) long when mature. A decorative, trouble-free species.

6. Abies procera

Blue Noble Fir

Height 60 m (200 ft). One of the tallest trees of the genus from the Oregon and Washington states, forming an erect, narrow pyramid. The cylindrical grey cones, up to 25 cm (10 in.) long are produced on trees when only some 6 m (20 ft) in height. The form 'Glauca' (illustrated) makes a large tree with pleasing blue-grey leaves, almost silver in the evening sunlight. 'Glauca Prostrata' is a charming low, spreading bush. A well-drained, moist, deep soil is best for these trees, which are unsuitable for chalk.

7. Abies pinsapo
Spanish Fir

Height 30 m (100 ft). An erect tree of the Sierra Bermeja, Spain. The leaves are arranged all round the stems like a bottle brush. The cylindrical cones are purplish-brown when young becoming fawn coloured and up to 15 cm (6 in.) long. This is one of the best species for a chalky soil. The form 'Glauca' (illustrated) makes a large tree with outstanding blue-grey leaves.

8. Araucaria araucana
Monkey-puzzle Tree or Chile Pine

Height 11 m (30 ft). Reaches a maximum height of 45 m (150 ft) in its native Tierra del Fuego. A bizarre tree making, when healthy, an egg-shaped outline of spreading branches sweeping down and then up; the branches are very prickly because they are encased in the spirally arranged, dark green, leathery, pointed leaves. The globular cones take three years to mature, by which time they are about 15 cm (6 in.) long, and of considerable weight. More widely planted in Victorian times and often too near the house. Comparatively quick growing in a moist, loamy soil.

9. Cedrus atlantica
Atlas Cedar

Height 15 m (50 ft). A handsome tree from the Atlas Mountains in Algeria and Morocco, which makes quick growth when young with ascending terminal branches. The 8 cm (3 in.) cones are greenish-yellow when young becoming violet-purple when mature. A magnificent tree for a spacious lawn or park where the soil is moist and well-drained. 'Glauca', the Blue Cedar (illustrated), with silvery-blue needles is more widely planted and is of outstanding beauty.

10. Cedrus deodara
Deodar, Cedar

Height 15 m (50 ft). An elegant tree from the Western Himalaya with horizontal branches, deflexed when mature and slender, pendent branchlets. The needles are blue-green when young becoming dark green. The bluish-green cones become pale brown when mature and are about 10 cm (4 in.) long. They are seldom produced until the tree is 30 to 40 years old. Not suitable for exposed positions but thrives in a sheltered sunny position and in a deep, loamy soil.

11. Cephalotaxus harringtonia drupacea
Cow's Tail Pine or
Japanese Plum Yew

Height 3 m (10 ft). A native of central China, Korea and Japan. Forms a dense shrub of compact habit. The dark green leaves have two white bands on the under surface. The fruit is olive-green pendent, pear-shaped and up to 5 cm (in.) long, technically a drupe. Prefer shade but will grow in sun and is no particular about soil.

12. Chamaecyparis pisifera
Moss Sawara or False Cypress

Height 9 m (30 ft). A broadly conic Japanese tree with horizontal branche forming flattened sprays of dark green the slender branchlets are marked wit white below. The 0·5-cm ($\frac{1}{4}$-in.) cone borne in clusters, green when young, becoming brownish-red. Not suitable for chalky soil. This species has given rise to numerous forms, among them the popular 'Squarrosa' (illustrated) bearing feathery sprays of glaucous foliage in the young stage. See also nos. 20 and 21.

13. Chamaecyparis lawsoniana
Lawson Cypress

Height 12 m (40 ft). A conical tree from California and Oregon with drooping branches. When established in a cool, moist soil and a sunny position it will make an annual growth of 30–60 cm (1 to 2 ft). It is lime tolerant. May be grown as a specimen tree and it is also useful as a hedge or screen. The little cones 0·7 cm ($\frac{1}{3}$ in.) long, are first greenish-blue, then brown, and freely produced. There are a large number of garden varieties in a diversity of form, some are imposing columnar trees and others are dwarf shrubs suitable for the rock garden. One of the best known is 'Allumii', Allum's Cypress (illustrated), with attractive blue-grey foliage borne in flattened sprays. Of dense growth and erect habit, it lends an air of permanency to a garden.

14. Chamaecyparis lawsoniana
'Aureovariegata'

Usually seen at a height of 8 m (26 ft). The flattened sprays of green foliage are marked with patches of pale gold, giving golden sheen in sunlight.

15. Chamaecyparis lawsoniana
'Fletcheri'

Height 6 m (20 ft). A handsome grey-green conifer which usually forms a multiple column. Fairly quick growing in the young stage.

16. Chamaecyparis lawsoniana
'Stewartii'

Height 8 m (26 ft). The elegant golden-yellow foliage makes this one of the most popular of the golden Lawsons. A tall tree of conical habit.

17. Chamaecyparis lawsoniana
'Triomphe de Boskoop'

Height 14 m (45 ft). A large, conical tree, vigorous in growth. The large sprays of glaucous-blue foliage should be trimmed in May or June to obtain dense growth.

18. Chamaecyparis nootkatensis
Nootka Cypress

Height 9 m (30 ft). From the coastal regions of Oregon to Alaska. The pendulous branches of dark green foliage have a rank smell when crushed. The blue-grey cones are about 1·5 cm ($\frac{1}{2}$ in.) long. 'Pendula', Weeping Nootka Cypress (illustrated), is a most graceful form with vertically swaying branchlets. An admirable specimen tree beside a lawn where space permits.

19. Chamaecyparis obtusa
Dwarf Hinoki or False Cypress

Height 8 m (26 ft). This Japanese tree is broadly conical in habit with branches spreading horizontally. The little cones are borne in clusters or solitary and are a beautiful blend of greyish-green and brownish-orange. In Japan it is valued for its timber. There are numerous dwarf varieties suitable for the rock garden including the very slow growing, miniature 'Nana' (illustrated), which may reach a height of 60 cm (2 ft) in about 20 years. It forms a dense dome of dark green foliage. Likes a moist, but well-drained, soil and a sunny position.

20. Chamaecyparis pisifera 'Aurea'

Height 6 m (20 ft). Similar to the species already described (no. 12), and needing similar soil conditions. The foliage of this Japanese form is golden-yellow in the young stage turning to soft green in late summer.

21. Chamaecyparis pisifera 'Filifera'
Thread Sawara, False Cypress

Height 6 m (20 ft). A form with long spreading branches and drooping whip-like branchlets of green foliage. There are several other forms including 'Filifera Aurea' which is smaller and slower growing with golden-yellow foliage.

22. Cryptomeria japonica
Japanese Cedar, Plume Cryptomeria

Height 15 m (50 ft). A fast-growing tree of columnar habit with spreading and decurving branches. The slender branchlets are pendent, green when young, becoming reddish. The bark is reddish and shredding. The small cones are globular. Grows well in moist soils. 'Elegans' (illustrated) makes a small tree with soft feathery blue-green foliage in summer, becoming red-bronze in autumn and winter.

23. Cryptomeria japonica 'Lobbii'
Lobb's Japanese Cedar

Height 15 m (50 ft). A slender tree with dense erect branches and deep rich green foliage. Thrives best in mild and moist districts in a moist humus-rich soil with a limited lime content and a sunny position.

24. Cryptomeria japonica 'Cristata'

Height 5 m (16 ft). A bush or small tree of conical form with curious flattened or fasciated secondary branches. Requires similar conditions to no. 23.

25. Cunninghamia lanceolata
Chinese Fir

Height 15 m (50 ft). A decorative tree from central and southern China with bright green leaves becoming bronze in autumn. Resembles the Monkey Puzzle (*Araucaria*) in habit. The rounded cones are borne in clusters of up to four in number about 4 cm (1½ in.) across. It requires an acid soil, not too dry, and a sheltered position as it is liable to damage by gales. In China the wood is used for making tea boxes.

26. Ginkgo biloba
Maidenhair Tree or Ginkgo

Height 30 m (100 ft). This unique conifer from western China is deciduous with unusual fan-shaped leaves which turn a clear yellow in the autumn. The male specimens have erect branches and pendent branchlets while the female tree has stouter horizontal branches and semi-pendent branchlets. The fruits are borne in pairs or threes. Its erect habit makes it an admirable tree as a specimen or for street planting as it does not object to town conditions. It will thrive in most soils.

27. Juniperus chinensis
Chinese Juniper

Height 8 m (26 ft). A native of north China, Japan and Mongolia. Of variable habit, the male plant being conical and the female having spreading branches. The leaves on mature plants are often elongated like a needle and on the young plant they are spiny. The little globular fruits are glaucous with an attractive white farina; they ripen in the second year. Junipers are slow-growing and will tolerate dryish and alkaline soils. The are diverse in form and the prostrate varieties are admirable for covering a sunny bank or on a large rock garden. There are innumerable garden forms of *J. chinensis*.

28. Juniperus × media (chinensis)

The hybrid 'Blaauw' (illustrated) is a vigorous juniper with ascending main branches up to about 120 cm (4 ft) with handsome blue-grey foliage borne in feathery sprays.

29. Juniperus × media (chinensis)
'Pfitzerana'
Pfitzer Juniper

Height 1 m (3 ft) with wide-spreading horizontal branches, drooping at the tips. Slow-growing, the spreading habit makes it invaluable for ground cover or for screening a man-hole cover. It may also be used in partial shade. An attractive sport of this variety is 'Pfitzerana Aurea' with terminal foliage suffused golden-bronze in summer.

30. Juniperus media plumosa aurea
Creeping Juniper, Golden Plume Chinese Juniper

From Japan, this makes an attractive carpet of glaucous green with a spread of 2·5 m (8 ft) or more when growing in a sunny position and in well-drained soil. At the centre the height is some 50 cm (20 in.). 'Aurea' (illustrated) has golden-tinged foliage in spring and summer.

31. Juniperus communis
Common Juniper

Height 3 m (10 ft). Widely distributed in North America, Europe, Asia, Japan. A native of the chalk downlands of southern England. A variable species usually of erect habit with spiny leaves 2 cm ($\frac{3}{4}$ in.) long, whitish above, green below.

The fruit is globular, about 0·5 cm ($\frac{1}{4}$ in.) across, green at first becoming blue. Indifferent as to soil so long as it is well drained and thrives in full sun. There are many garden forms including prostrate and dwarf varieties. 'Hornibrookii' (illustrated) is slow-growing and forms a spreading mat of glaucous green, the leaves being silvery-white beneath, sharply pointed and loosely spreading. It originated in County Galway, Ireland.

32. Juniperus communis 'Repanda'

Of Irish origin, this semi-prostrate juniper makes· a decorative ground cover plant in full sun. It is slow-growing and makes a pleasing green hummock.

33. Juniperus communis 'Hibernica'
Irish Juniper

Height 3 m (10 ft) or more making an attractive slender column of dense small needle-like foliage. Associates happily with heathers in full sun.

34. Juniperus communis 'Suecica'
Swedish Juniper

This is similar in habit to 'Hibernica' but the erect branches are more open and drooping at the tips.

35. Juniperus sabina
Savin Juniper

From southern and central Europe and Caucasus. A vigorous, semi-prostrate, dark green conifer of spreading habit with branches extending to about 2·5 m (8 ft) and slender, ascending branchlets. The small globular berries are bluish-black.

36. Juniperus sabina 'Hicksii'

Strong growing, semi-prostrate, with plumose grey-blue foliage borne on long branches with a spread of 2·5 m (8 ft) or more.

37. Juniperus sabina tamariscifolia

Spanish Juniper, Tamarix Savin Juniper

From the Pyrenees and southern European Alps. A handsome, compact juniper forming a low-growing, flat-topped shrub, bright green in colour. The horizontal branches have an eventual spread of 3 m (10 ft) or so. An admirable conifer for covering a dry, sunny bank or for a limestone rock garden where space permits.

38. Juniperus squamata

Nepal Juniper

Height 60 cm (2 ft) or semi-prostrate. A variable species from Asia, western Himalayas, China. A characteristic is the drooping tips to the leading shoots. The elliptical fruit is reddish-brown and about 0·5 cm ($\frac{1}{4}$ in.) long. This species which is not of much garden value has, however, given rise to some decorative varieties, in particular, 'Meyeri' (illustrated), a glaucous blue form of Chinese origin. This is a slow-growing, handsome juniper which may eventually attain a height of 1·5 m (5 ft) with outward spreading branches to 2·5 m (8 ft).

39. Juniperus virginiana

Pencil Cedar

Height 8 m (26 ft). A North American species of broadly conical habit with sharp-pointed, scale-like leaves. Fruit is brownish-purple, rounded 0·5 cm ($\frac{1}{4}$ in.) across. There are numerous desirable varieties. 'Elegans' (Elegantissima) (illustrated) has good foliage tinged with yellow. These junipers thrive in well-drained soil and prefer full sun.

40. Juniperus virginiana 'Glauca'

Height 6 m (30 ft). A dense column of silvery-grey scale-like leaves. The young bark is an attractive pink-purple. Makes a medium-sized tree.

41. Juniperus 'Grey Owl'

Height 1·5 m (5 ft). A hybrid of comparatively recent origin with silvery-grey foliage and widely spreading branches. A strong-growing shrub.

42. Juniperus excelsa

Variegated Spiny or Greek Juniper

Height 30 m (100 ft). From the Balkans, Asia Minor, Caucasus. Of loosely columnar habit with small grey-green leaves spreading at the tip. Tender in the British Isles and requires a sheltered position when young. Fruit spherical, about 1·5 cm ($\frac{1}{2}$ in.) across, deep purplish-brown and covered with a delicate waxy coating. 'Stricta Albovariegata' (illustrated) is a pleasing blend of green and pale cream foliage.

43. Juniperus horizontalis

Creeping Juniper.

Height 30 cm (1 ft). A prostrate evergreen from North America with long branches which eventually form a glaucous-green carpet, often turning purplish in winter. It has a spread of 2 m (6 ft) or more and is an admirable ground cover plant. Does quite well on poor gravelly soil and in sun. 'Glauca' (illustrated) has steel-blue sprays of slender foliage.

44. Larix decidua

European Larch

Height 30 m (100 ft). A sub-alpine species from the European Alps and Carpathians which forms a large tree, graceful, deciduous conifer with pale green dainty needles, turning golden brown before falling in autumn. The young cones are pink, becoming dark brown and up to 4 cm (1½ in.) long when mature. Widely planted for forestry purposes but charming as a specimen tree on a large lawn. Thrives on light dry soil and an open aspect.

45. Larix kaempferi
Japanese Larch

Height 18 m (60 ft) or more, resembling the European larch but the branches are stiffer and the shoots reddish, bearing bright green needles. The ovoid cones are about 2·5 cm (1 in.) long. Quick growing but susceptible to late spring frost.

46. Libocedrus decurrens
Incense Cedar

Height 21 m (70 ft). From the North American Pacific coast; usually of narrow columnar form, with dark green leaves on fan-shaped branchlets. The brownish bark peels off the trunk in narrow strips. Cones up to about 3 cm (1 in.) long, pendulous. A deep, moist but well-drained soil and a sunny sheltered position are the ideal conditions for this handsome specimen tree. Also known as *Calocedrus decurrens*.

47. Metasequoia glyptostroboides
Dawn Redwood

Height 30 m (100 ft) in its native land. Only introduced from China to the United States and Europe in 1947, having before its discovery in China been known only from fossils. This deciduous, fast-growing conifer makes an erect conical tree bearing feathery pale green foliage throughout the summer, becoming tawny pink in autumn. The warm reddish-brown bark of the trunk is attractive in winter sunlight. The cylindrical cones are up to about 3 cm (1 in.) long, pendulous. It makes a splendid specimen tree in moist, deep soil and in a reasonably sunny position. Young trees make 1 m (3 ft) or more of growth a year.

48. Picea abies (P. excelsa)
Common Spruce, Norway Spruce

Height 30 m (100 ft). From northern and central Europe, western Russia. Commonly called the Christmas tree. Narrowly pyramidal, with branchlets densely clothed with shining dark green leaves. Cones pendulous, cylindrical up to 15 cm (6 in.) long, purplish when young, but not borne until the tree is 30 to 40 years old. This tree is widely planted in Europe for forestry purposes and is useful to form a shelter belt. Thrives in deep, moist soil. Dry alkaline soils are not suitable for this imposing tree. There are numerous slow-growing forms suitable for a large rock garden.

49. Picea asperata
Dragon Spruce

Height 36 m (120 ft). From western China but similar in appearance to the Norway Spruce. Branches horizontal, opposite with shining green to greyish-green leaves in a close spiral. Cones up to 13 cm (5 in.) long, purplish when young. This species does not object to lime in the soil.

50. Picea glauca
White Spruce, Canadian Spruce

Height 11 m (36 ft). An extremely hardy tree from Canada and northern United States. Makes a dense tree of conical habit, most useful for planting in exposed places. The glaucous green leaves are densely arranged. The needles have an unpleasant odour when crushed and the trunk is covered with grey-brown bark. Cones are cylindrical, pale brown and up to 6 cm ($2\frac{1}{2}$ in.) long. Makes a better shelter belt tree for cold districts than the Norway Spruce.

51. Picea breweriana
Brewer's Weeping Spruce

Height 25 m (80 ft). A most elegant tree, broadly columnar, from the Rocky Mountains of California and Oregon, with spreading branches which ascend from the trunk. From these the slender branchlets hang like curtains to give a most graceful effect. The cones are cylindrical, pendulous, up to 13 cm (5 in.) long, green when young turning purple-brown as they mature. These are only borne on long established trees. Requires a moist, deep soil. There are few conifers that can match its elegance as a specimen tree on the spacious lawn.

52. Picea glauca albertiana 'Conica'
Height 1·3 m (4 ft). A slow growing dwarf from the Rocky Mountains, of dense pyramidal form admirable for a rock or heather garden. Thrives in well-drained soil and a sunny position. The soft foliage is bright grass-green.

53. Picea abies 'Nidiformis'
Height 30 cm (1 ft) with a spread of 1 m (3 ft). This slow-growing dwarf form of German origin makes a dense, flat-topped shrub with numerous horizontal branches. Particularly attractive when planted so that it can grow over a large rock or bank. The young foliage is light green at the tips.

54. Picea omorika
Serbian Spruce

Height 30 m (100 ft). A fast-growing slender tree from Yugoslavia, along the river Drina, with graceful, drooping branches curving upwards at the tips. Branchlets opposite with leaves dark green above, glaucous beneath. Cones cylindro-conical, 6 cm ($2\frac{1}{2}$ in.) long, bluish-black when young and produced on trees 5 or 6 years old. The young bark is an attractive orange-brown. Makes a beautiful individual specimen. Suitable for limestone or acid peat soils.

55. Picea orientalis
Oriental Spruce

Height 30 m (100 ft) on Black Sea coastal slopes, considerably less in cultivation. Habit pyramidal, with horizontal branches to ground level. Branchlets opposite, very short and densely arranged. Cones up to 10 cm (4 in.) long, slender, elongated, narrow at both ends, purple when young becoming greyish-brown. Once established in moist, well-drained soil, it makes quite rapid growth and is one of the best of the spruces in cultivation.

56. Picea pungens
Colorado Spruce

Height 11 m (36 ft) in cultivation. From Wyoming and New Mexico. An erect tree of conical habit. The rigid leaves are sharply pointed and arranged all round the branchlets. Cones cylindrical, up to 10 cm (4 in.) long, green when young becoming straw yellow, and persist until the autumn of the second year. The leaves have a pleasant smell when crushed. The various glaucous-leaved forms are much more popular and widely planted than the type.

57. Picea pungens 'Moerheimii'
Height 8 m (26 ft). A small, elegant tree with outstanding glaucous-blue, sharply pointed leaves on densely clothed branchlets.

58. Picea pungens 'Koster'
   Koster's Blue Spruce

Height 8 m (26 ft). Probably the best known Blue Spruce with intense silver blue needles. Makes a magnificent specimen tree for a focal point on a lawn.

59. Picea sitchensis
   Sitka Spruce

Height 40 m (135 ft). From California to Alaska in the coastal regions. Broadly conical, with branches in whorls. Leaves crowded, sharply pointed and spreading all round the branchlets. Cones 8 cm (3 in.) long, solitary, yellow-brown when young. The prickly leaves are pleasantly aromatic when crushed. It thrives in moist soil and is not a success in dry conditions. One of the most widely planted conifers used in northern parts of the British Isles for forestry purposes, where it attains a height of 20 m (65 ft). It requires a moist, cool climate and does not grow well in the eastern United States.

60. Pinus cembra
   Arolla Pine or Swiss Stone Pine

Height 8 m (26 ft) considerably taller in the European Alps, Carpathians, Urals and northern Siberia. Slow-growing, of pyramidal, dense habit. Leaves in fives, persisting for 3–5 years, borne on branchlets thickly covered in brown hairs. The egg-shaped cones are erect, short-stalked, 5 cm (2 in.) long, green when young becoming purplish-brown; only borne on mature trees. An attractive specimen tree with upturned branchlets to ground level.

61. Pinus contorta
   Shore or Beach Pine

Height 11 m (36 ft). From California to Alaska coastal regions. Of bushy habit with horizontal, slender twisted branches. Leaves in pairs closely borne along the branchlets. The conical cones are 5 cm (2 in.) long, usually in pairs, borne on quite young trees. A fast-growing, vigorous conifer which thrives in gravelly or sandy soils, but is not suitable for chalk. A useful tree for planting as a windbreak.

62. Pinus wallichiana (griffithii)
   Bhutan or Himalayan Pine

Height 14 m (45 ft). A broad-headed tree from the western Himalayas, with elegant, long drooping needles, in fives. The pendulous cones are banana-shaped, up to 30 cm (12 in.) long, solitary or in bunches of two or three at the end of strong growths. These cones are borne of trees about 15 years old and are purple-green, smeared with white resin. Tolerant of lime in moderation but not suitable for dry, chalky soil.

63. Pinus jeffreyi
   Jeffrey's Pine

Height 60 m (200 ft) in its native Californian coast regions. A magnificent tree with spire-like crown. Leaves in threes, up to 18 cm (7 in.) long. The terminal cones persist for a long time and are 15 cm (6 in.) long. The bark is one of the respects in which it differs from *Pinus ponderosa* with which it is often confused. *P. jeffreyi* likes a moist, light soil.

64. Pinus mugo
   (P. mughus, P. montana)
   Swiss Mountain Pine

Height up to 4 m (13 ft) in the central and south-eastern mountainous regions of Europe. Of variable habit, this slow-growing conifer makes a small, spreading tree or gnarled bush suitable for a large rock garden or wild garden. The rigid, curved leaves are borne in pairs. The conical cones are 5 cm (2 in.) long. Suitable for any well-drained soil and lime tolerant. There are several dwarf forms which are delightful in a scree or with hardy heathers.

65. Pinus nigra
Austrian Pine

Height 11 m (36 ft). Considerably taller in its native central and southern Europe. A fast-growing conifer with stiff leaves in pairs crowded in the branchlets. The rough bark is brown to dark brown and the cones solitary or in clusters up to 8 cm (3 in.) long. A useful shelter belt tree for dry, chalky soil.

66. Pinus parviflora
Japanese White Pine

Height 9 m (30 ft). A pyramidal tree when young with slender branchlets, becoming flat-topped as it matures. The leaves are borne in small tufts of five and the numerous cones are up to 8 cm (3 in.) long, very resinous. The bark is smooth. This pine likes a moist, well-drained loamy soil.

67. Pinus parviflora 'Glauca'

Height 9 m (30 ft). This attractive form has stiffer needles with a bluish-grey sheen.

68. Pinus peuce
Macedonian Pine

Height 11 m (36 ft). From the Balkan mountain tops, this hardy pine has densely borne needles in groups of five, and purple bark. The cylindrical cones are up to 13 cm (5 in.) long and persist for several years, becoming covered with white resin. Slow-growing and suitable for the smaller garden.

69. Pinus ponderosa
Western Yellow or Ponderosa Pine

Height 60 m (200 ft) in the western United States. This quick-growing, imposing conifer is indifferent to the type of soil as long as it is well-drained. The rigid needles, in groups of three, are borne on horizontal or drooping branches. The yellowish-brown bark peels off in long strips from mature trunks. Cones up to 20 cm (8 in.) long.

70. Pinus strobus
Eastern White or Weymouth Pine

Height 15 m (50 ft). A North American tree of conical habit with slender branches in whorls and thin needles in groups of five. The pendent, tapering cones are up to 15 cm (6 in.) long. A fast-growing, ornamental tree that likes a good loamy soil. The name Weymouth commemorates Lord Weymouth who planted this species extensively at Longleat, Wiltshire, England, in the early 1700s.

71. Pinus sylvestris
Scots Pine

Height 30 m (100 ft). The only native British pine, is also widely distributed from Spain to Siberia and North Asia. Usually a tall-stemmed tree, but occasionally with a twisted trunk and low spreading branches. The long needles are borne in pairs, and the small cones up to 8 cm (3 in.) long are in clusters. Thrives in dry regions with plenty of light and is not particular about the type of soil. There are numerous garden forms admirable for the rock garden.

72. Pseudotsuga menziesii
Pacific Coast or Oregon
Douglas Fir

Height 40 m (135 ft) on the mountain along the Pacific Coast of North

America. A fast-growing tree with deeply furrowed, corky bark on its straight trunk. The persistent leaves, arranged in twos, are aromatic when crushed. The pendent cones are green, becoming brown up to 10 cm (4 in.). A magnificent tree for cool, moist soil.

73. Sequoiadendron giganteum
Wellingtonia, Giant Redwood or Sequoia

Native to Sierra Nevada, California. A Giant Redwood is the most massive tree in the world, and indeed the vastest of all living things, with a circumference at the base of over 30 m (101 ft). With a height of 81 m (272 ft) it has an estimated volume of 50,000 cu ft and a weight of 1,065 tons. The oldest redwood felled was about 3,200 years old; by no means the oldest tree in the world but one in which the record of the annual rings (as in the plate) is very clearly displayed. There is a trunk section at Kew Botanical Gardens showing 1,335 annual rings and a smaller one at the Natural History Museum, London.

Of pyramidal form, it makes rapid growth and mature specimens have prominent buttress roots. The awl-shaped leaves persist for several years and are arranged spirally on down-swept branches. The ovoid cones are green, becoming reddish-brown, up to 8 cm (3 in.) long. A magnificent specimen tree which requires a deep, moist soil.

74. Sciadopitys verticillata
Umbrella Pine

Height 25 m (80 ft). A slow-growing Japanese decorative tree of unique appearance, with leaves spirally arranged along the branchlets. The short-stalked, ovoid cones are up to 10 cm (4 in.) long, green when young, becoming brown in the second year. Requires a lime-free soil and likes partial shade.

75. Taxodium distichum
Swamp or Common Bold Cypress

Height 30 m (100 ft). Considerably taller in its native south-western United States. Of pyramid form in the young stage, later becoming more spreading. The branchlets carry fresh green foliage which is deciduous and turns an attractive rusty red before falling in autumn. The globular cones are about 2·5 cm (1 in.) long, reddish-purple and resinous when young. A native of the south-eastern United States it thrives in moist or even marsh conditions and is an admirable hardy tree beside a river or lake; but it will grow in less wet soils.

76. Taxus baccata
English Yew

Height 12 m (40 ft). A native of the British Isles where it flourishes on chalky soils, forming a tree with wide-spreading branches, lives to a great age as is evident in many churchyards. Widely planted as an evergreen hedge, but as it is extremely poisonous it should not be grown where horses or cattle browse. The fruit consists of one seed surrounded by a round, bright red, fleshy mass known as an aril.

77. Taxus baccata 'Fastigiata Aureomarginata'
Golden Irish Yew

Height 4 m (13 ft). Forms an upright, broad column making it an admirable specimen for a focal point in the garden where the golden-edged narrow leaves show up well in the sunlight.

78. Taxus baccata 'Stricta' ('Fastigiata')
Irish Yew

Height 6 m (20 ft). An erect form of compact growth of the English Yew.

79.   Taxus cuspidata
Japanese Yew

Height 4 m (13 ft). An extremely hardy yew of shrubby habit. Similar to the English Yew but identified by the yellow tinge of the under-surface of the leaves. There are several slow-growing dwarf forms.

80.   Thuja plicata
Western Red Cedar or Giant Arborvitae

Height 10–15 m (33–50 ft), considerably taller in the Rocky Mountains. A fast-growing tree with spreading, supple branches and light brown to reddish shredding bark. The green cones become brown and are up to 2 cm ($\frac{3}{4}$ in.) long. Will withstand clipping and is useful for a tall hedge or screen. Can be grown in shade and on chalky soil. There are numerous forms including 'Aurea' with rich golden foliage.

81.   Thuja standishii
Japanese Arbovitae

Height 10–15 m (33–50 ft). Forms a wide pyramid with loosely spreading branches. The yellowish-green leaves are spotted white below and smell of lemon verbena when crushed. The cones are about 1·5 cm ($\frac{1}{2}$ in.) long. A useful tree for clay soils and reliably hardy.

82.   Thuja occidentalis
American Arborvitae

Height 9–12 m (30–40 ft). Native of eastern North America where it is an important timber tree. Of columnar habit, with horizontal upcurving branches and reddish-brown peeling bark. The pointed leaves are aromatic, and the cylindrical cones are green then reddish-brown, up to 1·5 cm ($\frac{1}{2}$ in.) long. It is extremely hardy and like other thujas prefers a moist, heavyish soil. There are numerous forms including slow-growing dense bushes suitable for the rock garden.

83.   Thuja occidentalis 'Ellwangerana'

Height 1·5 m (5 ft). A slow-growing, broadly conical bush. The golden variety 'Rheingold', also known as *T.* 'Ellwangerana Aurea', associates well with heathers, particularly with winter-flowering varieties.

84.   Thuja occidentalis 'Fastigiata'

Height 4 m (13 ft). Makes a dense column of compact growth admirable for a large heather garden.

85.   Thuja occidentalis 'Douglasii'

Height 6 m (20 ft). Forms a pyramid of dense foliage, with fan-shaped branchlets. An attractive specimen tree.

86.   Thujopsis dolabrata
Hiba, False Arborvitae

Height 3 m (10 ft), considerably taller in its native Japan. Related to *Thuja* but easily recognised by the silver-backed flattened leaves. A slow-growing, broadly conical shrub bearing globular cones, singly or in pairs, without stalk. Likes a sunny open position and a well-drained soil and is lime tolerant.

87.   Torreya nucifera
Japanese Torreya

Height 5–25 m (16–80 ft). A native of Japan which is very variable in cultivation. Of slender habit, the branches are in whorls becoming reddish-brown as they mature. The shining dark green leaves are aromatic when crushed. The oblong, fleshy fruit becomes purplish when ripe in its second year. Suitable for a warm, sheltered garden and a well-drained loamy or chalk soil.

88. Tsuga canadensis
Canada or Eastern Hemlock

Height 20 m (65 ft) taller in eastern North America. Forms an irregular rounded tree often producing several main stems from the base. It is the best species for chalky soil. The ovoid cones are up to 2·5 cm (1 in.) long and persist for some time. The wood is not resinous.

89. Tsuga heterophylla
Western Hemlock

Height 30 m (100 ft). A fast-growing, graceful spire-like tree from western North America. Extensively planted as a timber tree in North America and in Britain; also elegant as a specimen tree where space permits, but not suitable for chalky soil. The down-sweeping branches and semi-pendent branchlets bear many dainty, light green needles. The pale brown cones are about 2·5 cm (1 in.) long. Can be used for hedging purposes.

90. Tsuga diversifolia
Northern Japanese Hemlock

Height 10 m. (33 ft), usually less in cultivation, with horizontal spreading branches and slender hairy branchlets. The egg-shaped cones are 2 cm ($\frac{3}{4}$ in.) long. Of neat habit, it makes an attractive specimen tree for a lawn.

EVERGREEN TREES AND SHRUBS

91. Aucuba japonica
Variegated Japanese Aucuba,
Spotted Laurel

Height 2–3 m (6–9 ft). A useful Japanese shrub for shade and for town gardens in almost any soil. Tolerant of drips from overhanging trees. Plants of both sex need to be planted to produce the cheerful scarlet berries which are not usually eaten by birds. There are numerous varieties with variegated leaves, others with different leaf form, including 'Crotonifolia' (illustrated) also 'Fructu-albo' with yellowish-white berries.

92. Aucuba japonica 'Viridis'

Height 2 m (6 ft). The fleshy, glossy green leaves make this a useful shrub to brighten up a difficult shady corner.

93. Berberis buxifolia
Dwarf Magellan Barberry

Height 2 m (6 ft). This species from the Magellan Straits, Chile, is semi-evergreen and bears pendent amber-yellow flowers in late March and early April, followed by purple-blue berries. In common with other barberries it is easily grown in sun or partial shade in most soils so long as it is not water-logged. 'Nana' (illustrated), height 50 cm (1½ ft), is a slow-growing, compact evergreen form of rounded habit with purple foliage in winter. This dwarf is shy to flower.

94. Berberis candidula
Paleleaf Barberry

Height 1 m (3 ft). From western China, this dome-shaped shrub is of spreading habit and dense growth. The single, bright yellow flowers are produced in May followed by small blue-black berries. A decorative labour-saving ground-cover shrub.

95. Berberis gagnepainii
Black Barberry

Height 2 m (6 ft). An erect Chinese species with closely set stems and formidable spines. Makes an impenetrable hedge. The yellow pendent flowers appear in May and are much loved by bees, hence the usual crop of jet black berries. Thrives on chalk and other soils.

96. Berberis julianae
Wintergreen Barberry

Height 3 m (10 ft). The strong, spiny, dense stems of this Chinese shrub make it useful for a hedge or for screening. The spiny, toothed leaves are copper-tinted when young, and often colour in the autumn. The clusters of yellow flowers are followed by narrow black berries.

97. Berberis stenophylla
Rosemary Barberry

Height 3 m (10 ft). A vigorous hybrid which appeared at a nursery near Sheffield, England, in 1860 and is widely grown. Requires ample space as the arching branches have a spread of some 4 m (13 ft). In April and May the long, slender branches are covered with orange-yellow flowers. To form a hedge trim after the flowers have faded. The globular purple berries are not freely produced. Makes a decorative specimen shrub for an exposed site.

98. Berberis verruculosa
Warty Barberry

Height 1·5 m (5 ft). A slow-growing, compact Chinese shrub with arching, yet dense growths making it suitable for a low hedge. The yellow, pendent, scented flowers are produced in May and June and the black berries are covered with a blue bloom. Admirable as a specimen shrub growing on top of a bank where the branches can cascade gracefully.

99. Buxus sempervirens
Common Box

Height 3·5 m (11 ft). In the wild in southern Europe, north Africa and western Asia the Common Box varies from a large bush to a small tree. Easily grown in a reasonable soil, including chalk, this hardy shrub thrives in sun or partial shade. There are a great many different forms some of which are used for topiary and for hedging purposes. Often grown in tubs as clipped specimens which should never be allowed to dry out at the roots.

100. Buxus sempervirens 'Marginata'

Height 1·5 m (5 ft). Of erect habit with medium-sized, irregularly-shaped green leaves with pale yellow margin. Liable to revert.

101. Buxus sempervirens 'Aureovariegata'

Height 1·5 m (5 ft). Forms a dense bush with green leaves mottled or splashed creamy-yellow.

102. Buxus sempervirens 'Bullata'

Height 2 m (6 ft). An erect form of the Common Box with rounded, dark green leaves.

103. Calluna vulgaris
Heather, Ling

Height 20–40 cm (8–15 in.). Widely distributed on moorland and mountains of Britain, Europe and Asia Minor. The Heather of Scotland, the Ling of England. Easily grown in lime-free soil in full sun where it flowers in late summer more freely than in partial shade. Happiest in dry to moderately moist soil containing peat or leafy soil. Heather is a great asset to bee-keepers. Admirable for cutting for indoor decoration. There are a great number of named varieties some with double flowers, others with golden or bronze foliage, all of which are most effective when planted in bold groups in association with dwarf conifers.

104. Calluna vulgaris 'Alba Plena'
Height 30–40 cm (12–16 in.). An outstanding double white form flowering in September and October. Said to have been found in a marsh in the Netherlands.

105. Calluna vulgaris 'H. E. Beale'
Height 50 cm (2 ft). A splendid variety bearing long spikes of double rose-pink flowers from September to November. The original plant was found in the New Forest, England.

**106. Calluna vulgaris
         'Mair's Variety'**
Height 1 m (3 ft). A pyramidal bush with spikes of pure white single flowers in August and September. One of the best white heathers and admirable for cutting.

107. Calluna vulgaris 'C. W. Nix'
Height 60 cm (2 ft). Of upright growth with long spikes of dark crimson single flowers in September and October and attractive olive-green foliage.

108. Cotoneaster dammeri
Bearberry Cotoneaster
Height 5–10 cm (2–4 in.). A prostrate Chinese species with long growths trailing over the ground. Admirable for covering a bank or as ground cover beneath other shrubs. The largish white flowers produced in May are followed in the autumn by long-lasting red berries. In common with other cotoneasters, this thrives in almost any soil or conditions.

109. Cotoneaster microphyllus
Small-leaved Cotoneaster
Height 30 cm (1 ft). A very hardy Himalayan species with slender, rigid branches which makes it useful for covering a bank or rough ground. The small white flowers in May and June are followed by freely-borne scarlet berries.

**110. Cotoneaster salicifolius
         floccosus**

Height 4 m (13 ft). A graceful, arching shrub from China with willow-like leaves, silky white beneath. The white flowers in June are followed by clusters of red berries. It makes an attractive specimen shrub beside a lawn or near a pool.

111. Cotoneaster × watereri
Height 6 m (20 ft). A vigorous hybrid with spreading branches loaded each autumn with large clusters of scarlet berries which usually last well into the winter. It rarely fails in its prodigality. The white flowers are borne in large clusters in June and the dark green leaves are pale green beneath.

112. Cotoneaster 'Skogsholmen'
Height 60 cm (2 ft). A low-growing shrub of spreading habit bearing large, conspicuous coral-red berries in the autumn.

113. Daphne cneorum
Garland Flower or Rose Daphne
Height 30 cm (1 ft). A compact shrublet from central and southern Europe, lime tolerant but requires a moist, peaty soil. Can prove temperamental to establish. The crimson buds open as fragrant rose-pink clusters in April and May. A charming plant for a place on the rock garden shaded from the mid-day sun.

114. Erica × darleyensis
Darley Heath

Height 60 cm (2 ft). A hybrid between *E. mediterranea* and *E. carnea* which, unlike most heathers, does not object to limy soil but is not happy on shallow chalk. Of rounded, bushy habit the rose-pink terminal heads of flower are a delight from January to April. Most effective when grown with other winter-flowering heathers in a bold group.

115. Erica × darleyensis
'Silberschmelze'

Height 60 cm (2 ft). A first class white heather, 'Molten Silver' is a mass of fragrant flowers throughout the winter and spring. It originated as a sport from *E. × darleyensis* at a nursery in Wuppertal, Germany, in 1937.

116. Erica carnea
Alpine Heath

Height up to 25 cm (10 in.). *E. carnea* is a lime-tolerant native of the central European Alps where it is of prostrate growth and bears rosy-red flowers throughout the winter. There are many excellent named hybrids which form dense hummocks affording pleasing ground-cover throughout the year. A good medium loam suits these well. 'Vivellii' (illustrated) is one of the most beautiful with bronze foliage, deepening in the early spring, and deep vivid carmine flowers from February to April.

117. Erica carnea 'Winter Beauty'

Height 10–20 cm (4–8 in.). The bright, rich pink flowers are carried in abundance from December to March, forming low tufts of welcome colour.

118. Erica tetralix
Variety of Cross-leaf Heath

Height 20–30 cm (8–12 in.). *E. tetralix* is a native of northern Europe and the British Isles and bears dense heads of rose-coloured flowers from June to October. There are numerous named varieties, 'Alba Praecox' (illustrated) being a good, early white with dainty grey foliage. Thrives in cool, moist, lime-free peaty soil.

119. Erica vagans
Variety of Cornish Heath

Height 1 m (3 ft). *E. vagans* is a native of south-west Europe, including the British Isles, usually not far from the coast. Of spreading habit, with an eventual width of some 1·25 m (4 ft), it requires ample space. It prefers loam to peat, and does quite well on poor soil and will tolerate mildly alkaline conditions. The purplish-pink heads of flowers are at their best from August to October then the upright flower spikes turn brown and are still decorative. 'Mrs. D. F. Maxwell' (illustrated) is a deep cerise and one of the finest of many excellent hybrids.

120. Euonymus fortunei

A trailing evergreen which will also grow self-clinging on a wall to 3 m (10 ft). The pale green flowers in summer are followed by pink berries enclosing orange seeds. This Chinese species has given rise to several named forms 'Variegatus' ('Gracilis') (illustrated), has attractive greyish-green leaves with a white margin, sometimes tinged pink. An effective ground cover plant for sun or shade in almost any soil.

121. Euonymus fortunei radicans

Habit similar to no. 120. The leathery leaves are rather smaller than in *E. fortunei* and are shallowly toothed.

122. Euonymus fortunei 'Vegetus'

Height 1 m (3 ft) if support is available. A small bushy plant from Japan that is normally prostrate, with distinct broad, dull green leaves of thick texture.

123. Gaultheria procumbens
Checkerberry or Wintergreen

Height 6–15 cm (3–5 in.). A creeping North American species which is admirable for ground cover under trees where the soil is lime-free or on a peat bank. The small white or pinkish flowers in July and August are followed by a crop of cheerful bright red berries, which are most attractive with the autumn-tinted foliage. The new leaves are a translucent coral pink in the spring.

124. Hebe armstrongii

Height 1 m (3 ft). A New Zealand shrub, sometimes called *Veronica*, easily grown in well-drained soil and in a sunny position. The erect, dense branches have a whipcord appearance and in July milky-white flowers cluster at the tips of the golden cypress-like branchlets. Thrives in mild coastal districts.

125. Hedera colchica
Persian or Colchis Ivy

Height 6 m (20 ft). The strong-growing Caucasian species *H. colchica* has large, leathery dark green leaves up to 20 cm (8 in.) long. These self-clinging ivies are easily grown in ordinary soil and are quite happy in town gardens. 'Dentata' (illustrated) has even larger leaves, toothed, somewhat thinner than the type and of a softer green.

126. Hedera colchica
'Dentata Variegata'

Similar to no. 125 but much more ornamental with its conspicuous green and grey leaves with bold creamy-yellow margin. The leaves are not so

large as in the type but are most effective when growing on a patio wall, pillar or as ground cover in association with Periwinkle (*Vinca major*).

127. Hedera helix
Common Ivy

Height 15–30 m (50–100 ft). One of the hardiest climbers, native of the British Isles, Europe and Asia Minor. Useful for ground cover in shade but can become troublesome on walls. The glossy green leaves are variable, three- to five-lobed, often with silver markings along the veins. The leaves on the flowering shoots are entire. There are many forms differing in leaf colouring, shape of leaf and vigour of growth.

128. Hypericum calycinum
Rose of Sharon, Aaronsbeard or St. John's Wort

Height 30–45 cm (1–1½ ft). This native of south eastern Europe and Asia Minor is a useful ground cover plant for dry places in sun or shade. Tolerant of poor soil and drought, it carries golden-yellow flowers up to 10 cm (3 in.) across at the end of the shoots from June to September. Thrives in almost any soil, but to get the best results the old foliage should be clipped almost to the ground each spring.

129. Ilex aquifolium
Common Holly

Height 6–9 m (20–30 ft). In sun or shade, fully exposed to all the elements, or sheltered in woodlands, the Common Holly is widely distributed in Europe, including the British Isles, North Africa and Asia. Female trees bear heavy crops of red berries in a favourable season if a male tree is growing near-by. The berries are in great demand for Christmas decorations and are also consumed at

91-92   93   96 97   98

102   122   128   129

132 134 134

135 136 140-141

great speed by birds. There is a yellow-berried form. When planted as a hedge it becomes impenetrable. As a specimen tree, it is of pyramidal form and for such purposes there are numerous splendid varieties with variegated leaves, like no. 130.

130. Ilex aquifolium
'Aureomarginata Ovata'

Height 3 m (10 ft). The bold yellow margin to the leaves makes this a handsome Holly for a sunny position, or for a colourful hedge.

131. Ilex pernyi
Perny Holly

Height 3–5 m (10–16 ft). A distinct Chinese Holly with densely set, spiny, small leaves. Slow-growing, it forms a neat pyramid with yellow flowers followed by red berries.

132. Kalmia latifolia
Mountain Laurel

Height 2–3 m (6–10 ft). A splendid June flowering shrub from eastern North America that associates well with rhododendrons in a lime-free soil. The large, densely packed clusters of pink flowers and glossy green leaves make this an outstanding shrub in sun or partial shade. In a moist, peaty soil it will spread happily by means of suckers.

133. Lavandula spica (officinalis)
Old English Lavender

Height 1–1·25 m (3–4 ft). The Old English Lavender is, in fact, a native of the Mediterranean region and thrives in well-drained soil and a sunny position. The dense spikes of aromatic flowers and foliage are borne on slender stems from July to September and are a delight in the garden, useful for floral decorations and for *pot-pourri*. There are numerous named varieties in shades of lavender-blue, purple, pale pink and white. Decorative as a low-growing, but short-lived, hedge.

134. Ligustrum vulgare
Common Privet

Height 2–3 m (6–10 ft). This semi-evergreen native of Europe, including the chalky areas of southern England and North Africa was at one time much used for hedging purposes. It has been largely replaced for this purpose by the Japanese *L. ovalifolium* with larger oval leaves which are more reliably evergreen. The white, over-poweringly scented, flowers of the Common Privet are produced through the summer followed by black, oily berries. Will grow in any ordinary soil, in sun or shade.

135. Lonicera pileata
Privet Honeysuckle

Height 40–60 cm (16–24 in.). A low growing, semi-evergreen Chinese shrub with horizontal branches bearing small bright green leaves, small yellowish white fragrant flowers in May, followed by translucent violet berries. Suitable for ground cover in shade and does well near the sea in ordinary well-drained soil. The evergreen *L. nitida* is widely used to form a quick hedge and responds well to clipping.

136. Mahonia aquifolium
Oregon Grape, Holly Grape

Height 1–1·5 m (3–5 ft). Makes a dense carpet under trees but flowers more freely in a sunny, open position. The fragrant flowers appear in March and April, followed by tight bunches of blue black berries. This species from western North America often produce se layered branches where the soil is moist. Like other mahonias, this thrives in ordinary well-drained soil, including chalk. The foliage is useful for winter decoration.

137. Osmanthus heterophyllus
Holly Osmanthus

Height 2–3 m (6–10 ft). A slow growing, Japanese shrub with holly-like variable leaves, variegated in some forms, and small, white, fragrant flowers in autumn. A useful town garden shrub in almost any soil, in sun or partial shade, also thrives near the coast except in exposed gardens. Makes a good hedge, providing a dark background for more colourful plants.

138. Pachysandra terminalis
Japanese Spurge,
Japanese Pachysandra

Height 20–30 cm (8–12 in.). A useful ground cover plant from Japan which thrives in ordinary moist soil and in shade, even dense shade. Not suitable for shallow chalky soil. Of spreading habit, this carpeting shrub bears greenish-white flowers in early spring. There is a brighter-looking variegated form.

139. Pernettya mucronata
Chilean Pernettya

Height 1 m (3 ft). This South American shrub makes a dense bush bearing white flowers in May and June. It is, however, the large berries which are the main attraction lasting throughout the winter. They vary in colour from pink, red and purple to white. Requiring a lime-free soil, it associates happily with heathers and rhododendrons. Can be grown in shade but fruits better in sun. Plants of both sexes should be grown together to ensure fruits.

140. Pieris japonica
Japanese Andromeda

Height 2–3 m (6–10 ft). A Japanese species with shiny leaves which adds to its beauty in the winter sunshine. The young growths are an attractive copper colour. The wax-white flowers appearing in drooping panicles in March and April are pink in the bud stage.

141. Pieris 'Forest Flame'

Height 1–3 m (3–6 ft). A splendid hybrid with brilliant red young foliage in the spring, becoming pink and by June creamy-white to green. The white flowers are in large drooping panicles. The young growths are liable to damage by late frost, so choose a reasonably sheltered place protected by larger evergreen shrubs.

142. Pieris japonica
'Dorothy Wycoff'

This is a new American variety with red buds and pink flowers.

143. Prunus laurocerasus
Common Laurel, Cherry Laurel

Height 6 m (20 ft). The Common or Cherry Laurel is a native of eastern Europe and Asia Minor. It is mainly grown nowadays for screening purposes and is not suitable for modern small gardens. There are, however, numerous named varieties which make attractive garden plants in almost any well-drained soil and are suitable for partial shade. 'Otto Luyken' (illustrated), 1 m (3 ft) is a low-growing, compact shrub with erect stems bearing narrow, shiny dark green leaves.

144. Prunus laurocerasus
'Schipkaensis'

Height 2 m (6 ft). Of spreading habit, this very hardy variety flowers freely in

April and often carries a good crop of shiny black berries which are red before ripening.

145. Rhododendron ferrugineum
Alpenrose or
Rock Rhododendron

Height 1 m (3 ft). The rusty-leaved Alpenrose of Switzerland, the Pyrenees and southern European Alps. The attractive rustiness of the leaves is chiefly on the underside, and is due to a thick covering of rust-coloured scales. The small flowers are pink to crimson and they appear in June. Unlike most rhododendrons it is tolerant of some lime in the soil and is extremely hardy. A rounded bush when young but unfortunately it is liable to make straggly growth with age even for so small a shrub. There is also a white form. Closely related to *R. hirsutum.*

146. Rhododendron × halense
'Hardyzer Beauty'

Height 50–75 cm (20–30 in.). A hybrid between *R. ferrugineum* (no. 145) and *R. hirsutum* (no. 147). The variety 'Hardyzer Beauty' has quite large rich pink flowers in June. The leaves are without the golden-brown rust on the underside which is a feature of *R. ferrugineum.*

147. Rhododendron hirsutum
Tyrol Alpenrose or
Garland Rhododendron

Height 1 m (3 ft). The Tyrol Alpenrose is a hairy counterpart of *R. ferrugineum* and is found on limestone formations in the Alps but in cultivation it is better in an acid soil. The leaves are slightly scaly beneath and very hairy. The terminal clusters of small, tubular flowers open rose pink in June. This very hardy species has been in cultivation since 1656.

148. Rhododendron impeditum
'Moerheimii'

Height 30 cm (1 ft). The lavender-coloured, tubular flowers open in April and May. See no. 152.

149. Rhododendron russatum
Royal Alp Rhododendron

Height 50–100 cm ($1\frac{1}{2}$–3 ft). A slow-growing Chinese species of compact form, bearing dark violet funnel-shaped flowers in late April and May. The dull green leaves are rusty yellow on the under surface. Extremely hardy and a first-rate, free-flowering, leafy shrub.

150. Rhododendron
'Cunningham's White'

Height 2–3 m (6–10 ft). Raised in Edinburgh in 1830 and still one of the hardiest varieties, withstanding town conditions and smoky atmosphere better than most. The large, paper-white flowers with a yellow eye are borne in imposing trusses in May and June. In common with other rhododendron hybrids its main requirements are lime-free and reasonably moist soil.

151. Rhododendron 'Jewel'

Height 1·5–2 m (5–6 ft). The dark green oval leaves and large blood red funnel-shaped flowers make this an outstanding shrub in late May and June.

152. Rhododendron impeditum
Cloudland Rhododendron

Height 30 cm (1 ft). A slow-growing spreading Chinese shrub admirable for the rock garden with small grey-green scaly leaves. The flowers, which appear in April and May, vary in colour from pale mauve to purple-blue. Free flowering, it makes an attractive hummock and is extremely hardy.

153. Rhododendron wardii
   Ward Rhododendron

Height 2–3 m (6–10 ft). An elegant yellow-flowered species from China which makes a shapely bush with neat green leaves, blue-grey beneath. The large trusses of yellow bell-shaped flowers open in May or early June. This beautiful species does best in a reasonably sheltered garden and is the parent of several fine hybrids.

154. Rhododendron catawbiense

Height 2–3 m (6–10 ft). A North American species with dark green leathery leaves and funnel-shaped lilac flowers with green spots in the throat in May and June. The parent of some good hardy hybrids, it is closely related to the well-known purple *R. ponticum* but of hardier habit. 'Album' (illustrated) is an elegant white form.

155. Rhododendron catawbiense
   'Grandiflorum'

Height 2–3 m (6–10 ft). Bears large trusses of lilac-pink flowers in May and June.

156. Rhododendron 'Doncaster'

Height 2 m (6 ft). A slow-growing, hardy hybrid of *R. arboreum* with dark green, leathery leaves on erect growths. The brilliant crimson-scarlet flowers are borne in a close truss in May.

157. Rhododendron 'Hugh Koster'

Height 2 m (6 ft). A hybrid raised in Holland from the popular 'Doncaster', which it resembles in its sturdy habit but the glowing crimson flowers are not so intense in colour.

158. Rhododendron
   'Cunningham's Blush'

Height 2 m (6 ft). A very hardy hybrid bearing pale lilac-pink, funnel-shaped flowers in May to mid-June.

159. Rhododendron 'Davies Evans'

Height 1·5–2 m (5–6 ft). A rich purple, funnel-shaped flower with gold markings on the upper petal borne in a close truss. The colour in the bud stage is intense purple.

160. Rhododendron
   'Purple Splendour'

Height 1·5–2 m (5–6 ft). A very hardy *R. ponticum* hybrid bearing rich purple flowers in May and June with a prominent black blotch on the upper petal. Slow-growing and of compact habit, its colour is enhanced by growing a yellow or white variety nearby.

161. Rhododendron 'Caractacus'

Height 1·5–2 m (5–6 ft). An old variety seldom found in nurseries these days, nevertheless it is still a leader among the deep carmine hybrids with a neat, compact truss of well-shaped flowers.

162. Rhododendron
   'Madame Albert Moser'

Height 3–4 m (10–13 ft). A vigorous, hardy hybrid bearing freely large flowers in a close truss. The upper petal is heavily spotted yellow on a pale mauve-pink flower.

163. Rhododendron 'Pink Pearl'

Height 1·5–3 m (5–10 ft). Probably the best known hardy hybrid, raised in England, introduced in 1897 and still one of the most popular. Of upright growth, it bears its large, widely funnel-shaped flowers in a conical truss. Deep rose pink in the bud stage they open bright pink, fading to soft pink. The petals are attractively frilled.

164. Arundinaria japonica
Metake

Height 2–3 m (6–10 ft). A Japanese bamboo which forms a dense mass of growth with broad oblong leaves which are liable to have a 'burned' appearance in an exposed garden after severe weather. Of rampant growth, it is not suitable for a small garden but is admirable beside water or in partial shade in a woodland. In common with other bamboos it likes moisture but this does not mean boggy conditions. Bamboos take some time to get established and April is the best month to transplant. Avoid wind-swept sites.

165. Arundinaria murieliae

Height 2·5–3·5 m (8–11 ft). A beautiful Chinese Bamboo with erect, graceful, arching canes, bright green when young, ripening to yellow. The bright green narrow leaves appear on second-year canes. Ripe canes cut in the autumn are very useful for garden purposes. Closely related to *A. nitida*.

166. Arundinaria nitida

Height up to 3·5 m (11 ft). An elegant, hardy Chinese Bamboo with long, thin, delicate leaves, bright green above, grey-green beneath. The dark purple stems add to the charm of this clump-forming plant that likes dappled shade. The slender canes are also useful when cut and ripened for light-weight support for other plants.

167. Skimmia japonica

Height 75–100 cm (2½–3 ft). A slow-growing shrub from Japan tolerant of in-dustrial atmosphere, will grow in shade and in well-drained acid or chalk soils. Of dense habit, with leathery leaves and fragrant white flowers in April and May. These shrubs are, however, usually planted for their bright red berries which persist and are very welcome throughout the winter. As the male and female flowers are borne on separate plants it is necessary to grow one male in a group of female plants. There are also dwarf forms, both male and female, admirably suited to the small garden.

168. Stranvaesia davidiana
Chinese Stranvaesia

Height 3–5·5 m (10–18 ft). A vigorous Chinese shrub or small tree easily grown in well-drained loamy soil in sun or partial shade. Of umbrella-like form it bears many creamy-white hawthorn-like flowers in May followed by brilliant crimson berries on pendulous branches in September. Birds do not seem to relish the berries. Some of the leaves turn to shades of crimson in autumn. Less vigorous, *S. undulata* 'Fructulute' has bright yellow berries.

169. Vaccinium vitis-idaea
Cowberry

Height 15 cm (6 in.). A ground-hugging shrublet native of moor and woodland of northern Britain, as well as of Europe and North America. The leathery leaves are borne on wiry stems and bell-shaped white flowers, tinged pink, appear in summer. The small red berries are edible. Makes a useful ground-cover plant for shade where the soil is really moist. The curious specific name means 'Vine of Mount Ida' (Crete).

170. Viscum album
European Mistletoe

Height indefinite. A slow-growing parasite on a variety of trees and shrubs including apple, lime, elm, poplar, but rarely on conifers. A native of southern England, Europe and northern Asia, it eventually forms a dense pendulous cluster up to 1 m (3 ft) in diameter. The male and female flowers are produced on separate plants, the female bearing white semi-translucent berries from September to January. The berry contains one or occasionally 2–3 seeds surrounded by a sticky pulp. In nature the seed is spread by birds. To start a mistletoe plant oneself, a couple of seeds should be pressed well into an insertion made in the bark on the underside of a branch.

71. Viburnum × burkwoodii
Burkwood Viburnum

Height up to 2·5 m (8 ft). This hybrid has the pink-budded, fragrant white flowers of *V. carlesii*, which is one of the parents and the dark evergreen leaves, felted beneath, from the other parent *V. utile*. The clusters of flowers are borne from March to May. In common with most viburnums this thrives in a reasonably moist soil and, being early flowering, it is best grown where it is sheltered from the morning sun which can be damaging to the flowers after a late frost.

72. Viburnum davidii
David Viburnum

Height 50–100 cm (2–3 ft). A small, rounded bush of compact habit from western China, with conspicuous three-veined leaves. The flat heads of dull white flowers which appear in June are not particularly attractive but the turquoise-blue berries which follow certainly are during the winter. To encourage cross-pollination several plants should be grown in a group, otherwise a crop of berries is doubtful. Even without the berries this neatly-rounded shrublet is delightful as ground cover beneath other viburnums.

173. Viburnum rhytidophyllum

Height 3–4 m (10–13 ft). A fast-growing Chinese shrub bearing small, creamy-white flowers in May and June. The large, corrugated glossy-green leaves are grey felted beneath. It dislikes a windy site and shows its disapproval by torn and tattered leaves. It is necessary to plant two or more specimens to ensure a good crop of berries, which are red at first, finally black. Does well on chalky soil.

174. Vinca minor
Lesser Periwinkle

Height 5–10 cm (2–4 in.). A trailing European plant much used as ground cover in sun or shade and in poor dry soil. It has a long season of flower from March to July and intermittently until October. The stems root at intervals affording a ready means of increase. There are white-flowered forms, also deep plum-purple and one with variegated leaves.

175. Vinca major
Greater Periwinkle

Height 20–25 cm (8–10 in.). A vigorous trailing plant with ascending shoots, rooting as it spreads to 1 m (3 ft) or more. A native of central and southern Europe, it has become naturalised in the British Isles. The large purple-blue flowers appear from April to June and again sometimes in the autumn. It is an invasive creeper and should be planted with due consideration of its neighbours.

176. Vinca major 'Variegata'

Similar to no. 175 in all respects except that the leaves have a conspicuous creamy-white variegation. Cut sprays are useful for decorative arrangements.

169

143   144

145-148   154   158

164

165-166

167   171   172   173

EVERGREEN TREES AND SHRUBS HARDY
IN SOUTHERN EUROPE

177. Acacia cyanophylla
Blue-leaved Wattle

Height 4·5 m (15 ft). An elegant member of the very large acacia family, from Western Australia, with large, showy ball-like flowers which appear in spring. These are, in fact, tightly-packed clusters of perfect little flowers. Requires full sun and a well-drained soil, preferably lime-free. Remarkably tolerant of heat and drought. In all but the mildest climates wattles should be grown as cool greenhouse shrubs.

178. Camellia japonica hybrids

Height 2–4 m. (6–13 ft). The Common Camellia of Japan and Korea which used to be grown as a greenhouse plant has given rise to a large number of superb hybrids which are hardy enough to grow in the open in most parts of the British Isles. Easily grown in moist, lime-free soil and admirable for partial shade in light woodland or beside a north-facing wall. Flowering from March to May, the blooms are liable to damage by frost and plants should be sheltered from the early morning sun. Flowers are single, semi-double, double or of various other forms. The range of colour of the many beautiful named hybrids includes shades of red, pink, white, white flushed pink and other variations. They are decorative when grown in a tub, but careful watering is necessary so that the soil does not dry out or get frozen solid in a cold spell. Quite young plants produce flowers, not always true to type until the shrub is established.

179. Citrus sinensis
Sweet Orange

Height up to 6 m (20 ft). Of Chinese origin, this is the parent of the well-known edible Blood orange, the large Jaffa and other good varieties. A slightly spiny tree of rounded form bearing fragrant white flowers in May and June. Will withstand short periods of frost but is happier with a minimum night temperature of 7°C. (45°F.). Where such conditions prevail it may be grown in sunny position against a wall in a loamy, well-drained soil. Grown in a tub, it makes an attractive plant about 1·5 m (ft) high which can be stood in the open during the summer months and brought into a cool greenhouse in September. Fruits of the various citrus are borne on quite young trees.

180. Citrus limonia
Lemon

Height 2–3 m (6–10 ft). Introduced from eastern Asia and thrives in Mediterranean conditions. The fragrant white flowers, tinged red in the bud stage, appear in May and June. Requires similar treatment as no. 179 but appreciates a higher minimum winter night temperature, 10°C. (50°F.). Fruits usually take a year to ripen and have a variety of uses including oil from the peel used in perfumery.

181. Citrus nobilis (reticulata)
King Orange, Mandarin, Tangerine

Height up to 4·5 m (15 ft). This Chinese species is the hardiest citrus and makes a small, spiny tree with slender growths. The white flowers appear in May and June, singly or in clusters. The fruit has a thin, loose wrinkled peel and is about 5–8 cm (2–3 in) wide. Its requirements are similar to 179.

182. Cupressus sempervirens
Mediterranean or Italian Cypress

Height 18 m (60 ft) or more. A slender columnar tree, with ascending, resin-scented branches, which is a familiar sight along the Mediterranean coast. The cones, about 3 cm (1 in.) long, are greyish-green when young, becoming dull grey-brown. The wood is aromatic and is used in southern Europe for cabinet making. Requires a well-drained soil and a sunny position, and must be protected from frost and cold winds in exposed areas.

183. Eriobotrya japonica
Loquat

Height 3–6 m (10–20 ft). A slow-growing shrub or small tree from Japan and China with glossy, leathery leaves, 30 cm (12 in.) long, and deeply corrugated. The fragrant white flowers are borne in clusters resembling pear blossom. These appear during the winter and in mild climates edible fruit is produced. It is perfectly safe in south-west England and in sheltered places elsewhere. The best position is against a south-facing wall in well-drained, light loamy soil.

184. Eucalyptus globulus
Tasmanian Blue Gum

Height 60 m (200 ft). Possibly the fastest growing of all trees, recorded as having made 23 m (75 ft) of growth in 10 years in warm parts of America. In the young stage the mealy-white leaves are roundish, stalkless and on square stems, strongly aromatic. The mature leaves are dark green, gracefully curved and up to 45 cm (18 in.) long. In Britain, young plants are often seen in summer bedding displays, particularly in seaside parks, forming slender,

sparsely branched plants; they are easily raised from seed and are treated as annuals. The curious seed pods are rough and warty. Requires a well-drained loamy soil and full sun.

185. Jasminum floridum

Height up to 2·5 m (8 ft). A loose-growing shrub from western China which in Britain is best suited to a warm sunny wall and well-drained soil. The yellow flowers are borne in terminal clusters from July to September. If grown without support, it makes a semi-prostrate shrub of no great merit.

186. Laurus nobilis
Bay Laurel, Sweet Bay

Height 6–14 m (20–45 ft). This native of the Mediterranean region is frequently grown in a tub as a formal clipped shrub and in mild coastal regions it makes an admirable hedge, in ordinary well-drained soil. It is liable to damage by frost and bitter east winds in exposed gardens. The small yellowish-green flowers are borne in clusters in May followed by purple-black berries on the female plant. Does well in sun or shade. Bay leaves are used for flavouring savoury dishes, but should be used with care as the flavour is potent.

187. Myrtus communis
Myrtle

Height up to 3 m (10 ft). A native Mediterranean shrub cultivated in the British Isles since the 16th century, particularly in mild coastal regions. May be grown against a sunny wall in well-drained soil, including chalk, or will make an erect bush in a sheltered garden. The aromatic leaves and clusters of fragrant white blossom freely produced in July and August make this a popular plant. Used for wedding bouquets and decorative arrangements.

188. Myrtus communis 'Romana'
Similar to no. 187 but with larger leaves and more erect stems.

189. Nerium oleander
Variety of Oleander

Height 2·5–4·5 m (8–15 ft). A Mediterranean native of wooded valleys and ravines. In the British Isles it is most decorative when grown in a tub standing in the open in full sun in the summer and given cool greenhouse protection in winter. In sheltered gardens in south-western counties it may be grown in the open and is tolerant of lime in moderation. Flowering from June to October, there are single and double forms such as 'Flore Plena' (illustrated), with pink, red, cream or white blooms. Of erect habit, it is one of the most decorative shrubs in mild regions.

190. Olea europaea
Common Olive

Height 6–12 m (20–40 ft). A native of the Mediterranean region where it has long been grown commercially for the oil which is extracted from the fruit. Hardy only in south-west England where large trees may be seen in sheltered Cornish gardens. The fragrant, small white flowers are produced in July and August, or in May and June in its native conditions. Likes a loamy soil and full sun.

191. Phoenix canariensis
Canary Island Date Palm

Height 6 m (20 ft), or more. This species from the Canary Islands has an imposing head of slender dark green leaves about 5 m (16 ft) in length, and gracefully arching. In April small brownish-yellow flowers are borne in long panicles followed in mild climate by golden-brown fruits about 2·5 cm (in.) long. Fruits in the Isles of Scilly in a favourable season and is hardy in the extreme south-west of England in full sun and a well-drained soil.

192. Chamaerops humilis
Mediterranean Fan Palm

Height 3 m (10 ft) or more. A native of the western Mediterranean, including Algeria, which may be a small tree or more often have dense growths from the ground bearing fan-shaped leaves. The height of the plant and size of leaf vary considerably. The small yellow flowers are borne in a stiff panicle. Thrives in a heavyish well-drained loam and can be grown in the open in south-west England.

193. Jubaea spectabilis
Coquito Palm,
Chilean Wine Palm

Height 50 m (160 ft) or more. A species from Chile closely related to the Coconut Palm. The terminal crown of long leaves is spectacular. Flowers dark yellow and large roundish fruit with a hard-shelled nut. Requires a rich, sandy loam and a minimum winter temperature of 16°C. (61°F.).

194. Washingtonia filifera
California Fan Palm

Height 9–12 m (30–40 ft). A Californian species with an erect cylindrical stem topped with large spreading fan-like leaves beneath which are the remains of old leaves in a pendulous mass. The flowers are white. Treatment as for *Chamaerops* (no. 192).

195. Pinus pinea
Umbrella Pine or Italian Stone Pine

Height 12–18 m (40–60 ft). A conspicuous tree of the Mediterranean region with its flat or umbrella-like top. The long, bright green leaves are in pairs. The cone is up to 15 cm (6 in.) long and the quite large seeds are edible. These are not produced until the tree is some 30 years old. In Britain it is suitable for mild coastal regions and a sandy soil.

196. Pittosporum tobira
Japanese Pittosporum

Height 3 m (10 ft). A slow-growing species from Japan and China with attractive whorls of glossy green leaves and creamy-white, orange-blossom-scented flowers from May to July. An attractive wall shrub in southern England which is grown as a hedge in southern Europe. Likes a well-drained, fertile soil and will withstand drought.

197. Punica granatum
Pomegranate

Height 3 m (10 ft). A native of south-west Asia which is naturalised in south-east Europe. Slow-growing, of bushy habit, it bears funnel-shaped, scarlet to orange-red flowers from June to September. The edible fruits require a long, hot summer to ripen. It needs a well-drained soil and full sun. In southern England it needs the protection of a south-facing wall.

198. Quercus ilex
Holly or Holm Oak

Height 15–21 m (50–70 ft). A round-headed species from the Mediterranean and south-west Europe with leathery leaves, greyish beneath. In Britain it is reasonably hardy, doing especially well in coastal regions where the soil is well-drained. In June it is particularly attractive with its white woolly new shoots and yellow catkins. Tolerant of shade, it may also be grown as a hedge and withstands clipping.

199. Rosmarinus officinalis
Rosemary

Height 2 m (6 ft). An aromatic shrub from southern Europe and Asia Minor with blue flowers in May on erect stems. Thrives in full sun in any well-drained soil, including chalk. Sprigs of rosemary are used, either fresh or dried, for flavouring purposes. There are several named varieties, including a white form.

200. Viburnum tinus
Laurustinus

Height 2–3 m (6–10 ft). A strong-growing shrub from south-eastern Europe of dense, bushy habit flowering from late autumn to spring. The flowers are pink in the bud stage, opening white and are long-lasting. The berries are metallic blue, ripening to black. Does especially well in coastal districts and is tolerant of shade. A valuable winter-flowering shrub for all but the coldest districts.

INDEX OF LATIN NAMES

(Numbers refer both to colour plates and to descriptive notes)

INDEX OF ENGLISH NAMES

(Numbers refer both to colour plates and to descriptive notes)